Selected Prophecies of

NOSTRADAMUS

CHARTWELL
BOOKS, INC.

Published by
CHARTWELL BOOKS, INC.
A Division of **BOOK SALES, INC.**
114 Northfield Avenue, Edison, New Jersey 08837

ISBN 0-7858-1809-X

Typeset in Great Britain by Antony Gray
Printed and bound in China

CONTENTS

INTRODUCTION

FIVE HUNDRED YEARS after his birth, the Latinised name of French physician Michel de Nostredame still shines brighter than any other in the firmament of forecasters. Even in this century, whenever a notable event – usually a terrible one – occurs, many perfectly sensible people cannot resist wondering out loud whether Nostradamus might have predicted it.

The notion of predestination has been around a long time, but credible prediction of forthcoming events is relatively recent. Astrology, the association of the changing positions of planets and stars with the fates of individuals on Earth, probably seemed utter nonsense to the healthily sceptical of the ancient world and Middle Ages. But when Renaissance scientists started to reveal the heresy that our rotation within the solar system does indeed determine major events – night and day, tides, seasons, weather – the scepticism began to turn to wonder.

Nostradamus was born in 1503, at the height of the Renaissance, into a world already thoroughly reawakened to the pre-Christian wisdom of Aristotle and Plato – suppressed by a church anxious to protect its own teachings on creation and governance – and also alive to new disciplines including astronomy, botany and medicine.

These three great sciences were all within Nostradamus's grasp. He practised as a doctor, experimented widely with horticulture and was a noted astronomer. His interest in predicting future events was quite possibly no greater than that of any other polymath of his own or any other time.

Critics of Nostradamus might like to contemplate the revelation in 2003 that a later scientist, none other than Sir Isaac Newton, spent much of his long life (from 1642 to 1727) trying to determine when the world would end. Thousands of pages of Newton's notes on the biblical notion of Armageddon discovered in the Hebrew National Library in Jerusalem show that the greatest of English scientists had formulated predictions that the Second Coming of Christ would follow a series of plagues and wars. Newton even went so far as to write down the year in which God would finally ordain

Armageddon – in the year 2060. This is just two years in advance of the next appearance of Halley's Comet – in those days widely perceived as a harbinger of doom – in our skies. Astronomer Royal Sir Edmund Halley, who made the first-ever successful prediction of a comet's orbit, was also Newton's sponsor, and funded the publication of his seminal work *In Principia*.

In the enlightened England of King Charles II and his successors, Newton had less to fear from accusations of alchemy or sorcery than Nostradamus faced from the Inquisition of sixteenth-century France. But just as Nostradamus had done before him, Newton wrote his deliberations on God's purpose in a kind of code. He believed himself an 'adept' – someone ordained by God to interpret the secrets of His Creation – and that he must therefore reveal the unfolding truth in a manner that would be understood only to those of a like mind.

Although Newton's universe has always been seen as a mechanical one, governed by the laws of physics he so lucidly described, this unequalled scientist nevertheless invariably described the same universe as the creation of God. Newton was a man of unquestioning but comprehending faith.

Nostradamus was, similarly, a man both of belief and of wisdom. And if the revelation of Newton's deliberations serves to encourage a more balanced view today of the French seer's legacy to us, then so much the better.

Nostradamus wrote his famous *Centuries*, a series of four-line verses each believed to incorporate a distinct future prediction, in his middle years. First published in 1555, the quatrains are allegorical, camouflaged in references to the past and occasionally astrological. He claimed he could date each prediction, but refrained from doing so. Any dated foreseen event that came to pass in his own lifetime could have brought Nostradamus under suspicion of sorcery.

The Centuries are so-called because the complete work consists of individual volumes each comprising one hundred verses. It is known there were ten such volumes, but only about 940 quatrains have survived in manuscript. They have been transcribed many times, but they are certainly acknowledged as Nostradamus's work.

Nostradamus wrote down his prophecies as they came to him, and there is no pattern of time, place or events in the order which he ascribes to them. But many of them can be dated, and to make these remarkable verses as accessible as possible, this book arranges them in chronological order.

It is immediately apparent that many of the verses dwell on conflict, massacre and destruction, often involving kings. This has earned Nostradamus a reputation as a doom-monger. But it is vital to see these expectations in context. Throughout his life, Europe was at war as emerging nations battled to establish borders, dynasties, religious supremacy. Nostradamus's world was shaped by war, and he was right to see this pattern of life continue far into the future. Not until four hundred years after his death has France experienced a period of peace longer than thirty years. Long may it last.

Looking at his work from the twenty-first century, it is noticeable too how much of Nostradamus's language concerns overwhelming fire, explosion and the spread of man-made diseases. In the warfare of his own time, explosives were based in gunpowder, and were little more than propellants for gun and canon shot. But he seems to have visualised very well a post-Nobel period – three hundred years after his own – when nitro-glycerine and subsequent even more powerful 'high explosives' were to make warfare a very much more incendiary business.

It is all too noticeable that Nostradamus devoted no space to predicting peace in Europe or farther afield. Even in the post-Renaissance world, he foresaw no slackening in man's urge to find enemies and make war on them. And the seer does seem to be aware even of the cataclysmic world wars that lay far ahead in the twentieth century – and perhaps beyond.

Likewise with man-made diseases. Nostradamus was a doctor specialising in the prevention and treatment of epidemic diseases, notably the bubonic plague. He can have known little of infection – even that plague was usually parasite-borne – but seems to have looked ahead to a day when mankind had such control over diseases that they could be manipulated, even as weapons of war.

But most immediately impressive are Nostradamus's expectations of events that were to take place in his own lifetime. True, he did camouflage them to keep himself out of the clutches of the Inquisition – but with hindsight, the disguise is very thin. It was one such prediction that brought

Nostradamus to the close attention of the French court, and thus of the world.

Henri II, King of France from 1547, died on 10 July 1559 in a manner clearly foretold by Nostradamus four years previously. In a joust, the king was wounded through his visor in the eye by a young officer of his guard. The king lingered for ten agonised days before he succumbed. Nostradamus's warning had been read in advance of the event, possibly even by the king himself, and certainly by his consort Catherine de Medici. Nostradamus was known to the Queen, who had invited him to Court in 1556 and consulted him about her children's futures. The prophet's acquaintance with Catherine probably saved his life, because there were calls for his arrest as a magician. On the Queen's clear instruction, Nostradamus was left alone.

Thus did the name Nostradamus find a place in history. By the time he died in 1566 many of his predictions had come palpably true. And in the hundreds of years since, the accuracy of his forecasting has continued to intrigue succeeding generations.

Can we guess how he did it? There is certainly no doubting

Nostradamus's sincerity. A religious man, he believed himself to be an adept, an heir to the traditions of alchemy, just as Isaac Newton did more than a century later. He saw it as his task responsibly to transcribe the secrets of the natural world as a warning to mankind.

But it seems likely too that Nostradamus's political nous must have played a part. As a natural scientist and a well-travelled physician in regular contact with the leading thinkers of his own time, he was certainly well placed to look ahead. Given the tyrannies that passed for governments in Europe before and during Nostradamus's time, for example, his foreseeing of events such as the French Revolution do not necessarily seem all that remarkable.

But what is remarkable is that Nostradamus actually committed himself to these predictions and published them. He must have known that his words would cause scorn and disbelief to be heaped on him, but he cared enough about what he had to say to stand by his words for all his life.

There is much in that life that makes sense of the uses to which Michel de Nostredame put his sixty-three years.

He was born on 14 December 1503 in St Rémy, Provence, into a family of Jews who had adopted the name Nostredame – an overt dedication to Our Lady no doubt adopted by many of the newly converted – at the time of their forced conversion to Catholicism five years before Michel's birth. New French king Louis XII had issued an edict that all non-Catholics among his subjects must be baptized into the Church or face exile.

Jacques de Nostredame, Michel's father, was a well-to-do lawyer and the boy certainly enjoyed a comfortable upbringing, and a liberal education. Much of his learning has been attributed to his two grandfathers, Pierre de Nostredame and Jean de St Rémy, both former physicians to René, Duke of Anjou and Count of Provence and Piedmont. Latterly known as René the Good, he had been an enlightened ruler tolerant of the Jews, to whom he gave refuge from Catholic persecution in Spain. It is possible that both of Nostradamus's grandfathers had been among those Spanish exiles.

René devoted the last of his years to the poetry of Provence, earning the romantic soubriquet the Last of the Troubadours, and died in 1480 without a surviving male heir (his daughter Margaret of Anjou had married Henry VI of England). It seems likely Nostredame and St Rémy, who took his name from the town where he settled, accompanied the court to Provence. But disputes over René's legacy led to the annexation of Provence by the French crown in 1486 and the region lost the last of its religious freedoms with Louis XII's edict of 1498.

Young Michel received both a classical education and Jewish teachings in the natural sciences of a kind still forbidden to Christians. As well as mastering Latin, Greek and ancient history, the boy learned from his grandfather Jean de St Rémy the practices of medicine, chemistry and astronomy. These three disciplines were closely linked. It is hard now to understand that five hundred years ago the ingredients of pharmacology were planted and harvested in accordance with the configurations of the stars in the sky, but this was the mainstream medical practice of the day – and Michel proved to have a natural aptitude for it.

The family were left in no doubt that medicine was the boy's *metier*, and Michel was sent to college in Avignon to study the prescribed course of grammar, rhetoric and philosophy. He distinguished himself in astronomy above all. Jean-Aimé de Chavigny, later a student of Nostradamus and his first biographer, records that young Michel would explain to fellow students that the Earth was like a ball and that it 'revolved each year around the Sun' each day exposing one hemisphere then the other to the Sun's light. This was fifty years before Galileo was even born.

In 1520 plague struck Avignon and Nostradamus fled the city. But he did not return home. Instead, he seems to have decided to follow in the footsteps of a personal hero, the itinerant German physician Paracelsus. Just ten years the young man's senior, Paracelsus was making groundbreaking medical discoveries in his journeys through Europe and the Near East.

For the next eight years, Nostradamus travelled to unknown destinations and is lost to history until October 1529, when he enrolled in the medical school at Montpellier, the most distinguished faculty in France. By 1533 he had graduated and set up a home and a practice in Agen. But again, plague struck. His wife and two children were among the victims.

Again, Nostradamus took to the road. He is believed to have worked in Bordeaux, Carcassonne, Toulouse and other cities, but never to have settled for a long period in any one place.

He specialised in treating plague diseases and it is at Marseilles in 1544, amidst the outbreak there, that he really returns to the light. He studied at Marseilles under the leading doctor Louis Serres, and soon came into demand throughout Provence in his own right for his ability to manage plague outbreaks, not only treating individual patients, but advising on prevention, hygiene, diet.

In the town of Salon, Nostradamus met a young widow, Anne Ponsarde. On 11 November 1547, they married and moved into a house in the rue Ferreiraux – now rue Nostradamus. But now, again, the physician set out on his travels, this time for Italy.

His destination was the cradle of the Renaissance, Florence. It seems by now Nostradamus had found his second *métier*. He knew he could foretell events, and he sought to discover the precedents for his power. In Renaissance Italy he would be able to devour the teachings of the classical world, of the occult, so long suppressed by the Church.

It was in Italy in 1548 that one of the early legends of Nostradamus's powers arises. At Ancona in the Marches he is said to have encountered a young Franciscan friar and to have fallen to his knees in front of him. To the friar's enquiry he replied: 'I am in the presence of the Holy Father.' The incident was well remembered by the Franciscan, Felix Peretti, who became Pope Sixtus V in 1585.

Nostradamus seems to have continued on his Italian travels to practise medicine, but records of his visits to cities including Venice, Milan and Naples – resting place of Virgil, the Roman poet who predicted the Messiah – concern his achievements as a seer, not as a doctor.

In 1555 his *Centuries* were published. He probably began work on them in the *astrologerie* he added to the Salon house five years earlier. Jean-Aimé Chavigny, a pupil, later wrote that Nostradamus had 'hesitated for a long time to publish them, realising their revelations would certainly attract harsh criticism and mockery'. But Chavigny added that when the verses did go into print 'immediately, news of his words spread by word of mouth through France and beyond, with great wonder'.

Nostradamus prefaced the first edition with an introduction dedicated to his baby son César, the embodiment of the future. But the seer expressed little faith that his words would be heeded. 'For long I have been foretelling what will come to pass,' he wrote, but had been reluctant to commit himself, 'knowing that rulers and religions will scorn what subsequent centuries will find to be true.'

Prefacing the second edition of the prophecies, Nostradamus went further. He dedicated the volume to Henri II, reiterating that, as he had said in the first, his verses were a code, but adding that, had he wished, he could have dated every single prophecy – but avoided doing so for fear of being called a sorcerer.

The Centuries brought Nostradamus to the attention of the court. Catherine de Medici was a follower of the occult and summoned him to Paris in July 1556. It is known the seer had several interviews with her. He became a figure at court, besieged by its members for medical remedies and, of course, horoscopes.

Some evocative stories arose from this period in Nostradamus's life. One concerned a boy in the service of the Beauveau family who knocked, late at night, at the seer's door. The youth had been sent with a request from the family but on his way had lost the dog he had brought with him and spent hours looking for it. Without opening the door, Nostradamus answered the knock by calling: 'Don't worry about the lost dog. Go and look on the Orléans road and you'll find it there tied up.' The page duly found the animal, and the story was all round Paris by the morning.

Nostradamus's major royal assignment was at Blois, private home of Henri II and Catherine's seven children, where he was asked to cast their horoscopes. These have not survived, but many of the verses in *The Centuries* give clues to the fates of the royal children. Three of them became kings of France – but six of the seven died sadly young.

The prophet's royal interlude ended suddenly. A lady, later described by Nostradamus as 'a very honest woman' tipped him off that the Paris Justices were planning to question him as to the nature of his occupation. They would require him to explain that he was neither a miracle-worker nor a fake. Nostradamus, well aware of the witch-finder's methods, fled back to Salon.

He returned with the rewards of his time at court and settled down to a contented life. He and Anne had six children. He became involved in local politics and good works. He dispensed wisdom as well as medicines and horoscopes, and enjoyed his fame.

His powers were, inevitably, put to the test. One story is of his stay at the Château de Fains in Lorraine, as a guest of the sceptical Comte de Florinville. Inspecting the home farm, the count selected a pair of piglets, one black and one white, challenging Nostradamus to predict their futures. 'You will eat the black, and a wolf will consume the white,' said the seer.

The count naturally instructed his cook to prepare the white piglet for dinner that night. But in the afternoon a wolf cub kept as a pet in the castle crept into the kitchen and made off with the carcass. The cook could do nothing other than to replace the purloined white piglet with the black one. Once cooked, he reasoned, the count would not know.

At the meal, Florinville told Nostradamus his prophecy

was void, for this was the white piglet. But no, the seer replied, it is the black one. The cook was summoned and when he could not produce the black piglet, Nostradamus was vindicated. Not so the cook.

Nostradamus lived to be sixty-three. He received the last rites on the evening of 1 July 1566 and died during the night. Anne lived on sixteen years and was buried alongside him in the Franciscan chapel at Salon. The inscription she had placed over the graves remains to this day. It reads: 'Into Almighty God's hands I commend the remains of illustrious Michel de Nostredame, alone judged by mortal men to describe in near-divine words the events of the whole world under the influence of the stars.'

Predictions for the
21st CENTURY –
AND BEYOND

L'horrible peste Perynte et Nicopolle,
Le Chersonnez tiendra et Marceloyne,
La Thessalie vastera l'Amphipolle,
Mal incogneu et le refus d'Anthoine.

The terrible plague at Perinthus and Nicopolis
Will strike both the peninsular and Macedonia
It will devastate Thessaly and Amphipolis
An unknown evil; a refusal by Anthony.

All the places mentioned can be located either in Greece or in the former Yugoslavian republic of Macedonia. The century began with war in the region and future trouble in the Balkans can never be ruled out. The reference to 'Anthony' might fancifully be associated to the name of a key international player in this theatre of war, Anthony Blair, British Prime Minister.

⌛ 2000 ⌛

Mars et Mercure et l'argent joint ensemble,
Vers le midi extreme siccité
Au fond d'Asie on dira terre tremble,
Corinthe, Ephese lors en perplexité.

Mars, Mercury and the Moon will join forces
Causing a terrible drought in the south
It will seem as if the earth trembles in Asia
And both Corinth and Ephesus will be troubled.

The first conjunction indicated in line 1 took place in July 2000, presaging a series of disasters beginning with drought in Africa and culminating with troubles between Greece and Turkey, symbolising the Christian and Muslim worlds.

⧗ 2001 ⧗

Jardin du monde au pres du cité neufve,
Dans le chemin des montaignes cavees,
Sera saisi et plongé dans la Cuve,
Beuvant par force eaux soulfre envenimees.

Wilderness comes close to reclaiming the new city
In the roadway, between the hollow mountains
It will be seized, and plunged into the vat
Drinking, in desperation, the sulphur-poisoned waters.

Lines that have inevitably been drawn into association with the
events of 11 September 2001. Nostradamus appears to foresee the
skyscrapers of New York, calling them hollow mountains. The
World Trade Centre was destroyed by two aircraft hijacked by
Muslim terrorists, the twin towers collapsing into the under-
ground void on a site now known as Ground Zero. The city's
seaboard location is suggested by the sulphurous waters.

Mars et le sceptre se trouvera conjoinct,
Dessoubz Cancer calamiteuse guerre
Un peu apres sera nouveau Roi oingt,
Qui par long temps pacifiera la terre.

Mars and the sceptre will join
There will be a calamitous war under Cancer
Soon afterwards, a new king will be anointed
Who will bring long term peace to the earth.

Nostradamus warns of conflict early in the third millennium, lasting until a new leader restores peace.

2003

Soubs l'opposite climat Babylonique,
Grand sera de sang effusion
Que terre et mer, air, ciel sera inique,
Sectes, faim, regnes, pestes, confusion.

In a non-Babylonian climate
There will be much bloodshed
Land, sea, heaven and air will seem unjust
Sects, hunger, new kingdoms, plagues and
    confusion will follow.

A vivid portrayal of the conditions of the Iraqi conflict of 2003.
Of course, it may refer to previous wars in the region – or future
ones.

⧗ 2004 ⧗

L'horrible guerre qu'en l'occident s'apreste
L'an ensuivant viendra la pestilence,
Si fort horribles que jeune, vieux, ne beste,
Sang, feu, Mercure, Mars, Jupiter en France.

The terrible war being prepared in the West
Will be followed, one year later, by a plague
Of such virulence it spares neither young,
    old, nor animal
Blood, fire, Mercury, Mars, Jupiter in France.

War waged by Western powers, followed a year later by an epidemic. The conjunction in line 4 could indicate September 2004.

Un grand d'Auxerre mourra bien miserable,
Chassé de ceux qui soubs lui ont esté
Serré de chaines, apres d'un rude cable,
En l'an que Mars, Venus, et Sol, mis en esté.

A great man from Auxerre will die in poverty
Driven out by his own underlings
Bound in chains, at the end of a rough rope
In the year in which Mars, Venus and the Sun
    conjoin in summer.

This conjunction next arises in June to July 2006. The great man
could be a political leader toppled for his crimes.

⧗ 2006 ⧗

Avant qu'à Rome grand aie rendu l'ame
Effrayeur grande à l'armée estrangere
Par Esquadrons, l'embusche pres de Parme
Puis les deux rouges ensemble feront chere.

Before the great man dies at Rome
There will be much terror for the foreign army
An ambush, by squadrons, near Parma
Then the two red ones will hold a joint celebration.

The Pope is dying, and northern Italy (signified by Parma) is in
a state of conflict. This is good news to two rebels. A harbinger
of a north-south split in Italy, plotted by factions in both halves
of the country, soon after the death of the present Pope?

Dedans Tholoze non loing de Beluzer
Faisant un puis long, palais d'espectacle
Tresor trouvé un chacun ira vexer
Et en deux locz et pres del vasacle.

In Toulouse, not far from Beluzer
Making a deep pit, a palace of spectacle
A found treasure will upset everyone
Both in two locations and near the Basacle.

The Latin proverb *habet aurum Tolosanum,* 'he has the gold of Toulouse' and signifying ill-gotten gains, has for 1500 years fostered the belief that in this great city of southern France lies a vast treasure waiting to be discovered. Nostradamus's treasure map is as cryptic as might be expected. There is a local myth that the treasure was looted by Clovis, conqueror of Roman Gaul, from Toulouse in 507.

Sur les rochers sang on les verra plouvoir,
Sol Orient, Saturne Occidental
Pres d'Orgon guerre, à Rome grand mal voir,
Nefs parfondrees et prins le Tridental.

Blood will rain on the rocks
The Sun in the East, Saturn in the West
War will occur near Orgon, and great evil near Rome
Ships will be broached, and the land of the Trident
    taken.

The Trident could refer to the sea-god Poseidon, who wielded one, and was renowned for sending earthquakes and plagues against his enemies. A presage of a major disaster, it is striking in this verse that both Trident and Poseidon are names taken by current nuclear-powered submarines.

Le grand monarque que fera compagnie,
Avec deux rois unis par amitié
O quel soupir fera la grand mesgnie,
Enfans Narbon à l'entour quel pitié.

The great monarch who will join
With two kings, united in friendship
O how his people will moan
What sadness for the Narbonnais.

The European Union brought together France's president and the 'kings' of Luxembourg and Monaco, both of whom France supplies with nuclear generated electricity from the Rhone valley. 'Narbonne', which is situated on the Mediterranean coast opposite the mouth of the Rhone river, would be one of the worst sufferers in any ensuing nuclear disaster.

⧖ 2011 ⧖

Pau, Verone, Vicence, Sarragousse,
De glaives loings terroirs de sang humides.
Peste si grande viendra à la grand gousse,
Proche secours, et bien loing les remedes.

Pau, Verona, Vicenza and Saragossa
Their swords damp with the blood of distant lands
Will suffer an evil plague, borne by a shell
Relief may be near, but the remedies are far away.

France, Italy and Spain – symbolising the great powers – will be
struck by a terrible virus 'borne by a shell'. This is one of a number
of quatrains that appear to foretell the onset of a chemical war – a
grimly real prospect in the twenty-first century.

⧖ 2011 ⧖

Les dieux feront aux humains apparance,
Ce qu'ils seront auteurs de grand conflict
Avant ciel veu serein espee et lance,
Que vers main gauche sera plus grand afflit.

The gods will fool mankind, making out
That they are the authors of a great war
Once, the sky was free of hardware
But now, on the left, there will be great damage.

Foretelling war between the West and China. The United States
lies 'on the left' of the world map, China on the right. The US
will suffer grievous casualties. The gods fool mankind into over-
populating the earth, triggering Chinese military aggression.

☒ 2012 ☒

L'ire insensee du combat furieux
Fera à table par freres le fer luire
Les despartir, blessée, curieux
Le fier duelle viendra en France nuire.

The senseless rage of a furious war
Will cause brothers to unsheathe their swords at table
They are separated, wounded, curiously cured
The proud duel will cause harm to France.

The break-up of the European Union. Turkey's successful admission has prompted Greece, supported by Italy, to threaten withdrawal. In the ensuing economic chaos, France is the principal loser.

Le camp Ascap d'Europe partira,
S'adjoignant proche de l'isle submergée
D'Arton classe phalange pliera,
Nombril du monde plus grand voix subrogée.

The aimless army will leave Europe
Meeting once more near the submerged island
The ranks of the d'Arton fleet will collapse
And a new world centre, with a greater voice,
        will be substituted.

This could foretell the end of Nato, or OTAN (d'Arton) as it is known in France. Russia is already putting pressure on the members of Nato, now including former Warsaw Pact states, to disband, and create a new alliance that better reflects the makeup of the post Cold War world.

Le prince rare de pitié et clemence,
Viendra changer par mort grand cognoissance
Par grand repos le regne travaillé,
Lors que le grand tost sera estrillé.

A prince of rare pity and clemency
Will change and gain great knowledge through death
The kingdom will thrive in tranquillity
However the great man will soon be fleeced.

When the Prince of Wales becomes King the tribulations of his
earlier life will stand him in good stead. The kingdom will enjoy
peace and prosperity, but the monarch may have to beware
those close to him.

La grande famine que je sens approcher,
Souvent tourner, puis estre universelle
Si grand et long qu'un viendra arracher,
Du bois racine et l'enfant de mamelle.

The great famine which I see approaching
Will start sporadically, slowly becoming universal
It will be so great, and last so long, that roots
Are torn up, and babies from their mothers' breast.

A quarter of a million people are born on the planet every day. If this birth rate continues, the population of the world will reach eight billion by 2020. Without intervention, plant life will be insufficient to support human life and there will be insufficient drinking water for all.

⧗ 2022 ⧗

Qu'en dans poisson, fer et lettres enfermée
Hors sortira qui puis fera la guerre
Aura par mer sa classe bien ramée
Apparoissant pres de Latine terre.

When weapons and letters are sealed in a fish
A war-maker will come
His fleet will have travelled far
They will appear near the Latin shore.

Military orders carried in a submarine. British and US nuclear-powered submarines can circumnavigate the globe, and carry sealed orders to be opened when signals are received from on-shore commandeers. Individual boats carry sufficient atomic warheads to devastate entire nations.

⧗ 2026 ⧗

Tant attendu ne reviendra jamais
Dedans l'Europe, en Asie apparoistra
Un de la ligue issu du grand Hermes
Et sur tous rois des orientz croistra.

Eagerly awaited, he will never go back
To Europe, but will reappear in Asia
One of the many descendants of great Hermes
He will rise above all other kings of the Orient.

Hermes is Hermes Trismegistus, otherwise known as the Egyptian god Thoth, author of numerous works on alchemy, magic and astrology. A new spiritual leader or Messiah, to follow on from Jesus Christ, will appear in the East. Elsewhere Nostradamus tells us this new Messiah will be born at the exact moment in which the sun is blotted out from the earth during the eclipse of 11 August 1999. He will come into his own twenty-seven years later, and will be instrumental in bringing to an end the long-running global conflict that will have started around the time of his birth.

La foi Punicque en Orient rompue
Grand Jud. et Rosne, Loire et Tag changeront.
Quand du mulet la faim sera repue,
Classe espargie, sang et corps nageront.

Libyan treachery breaks out in the east
The river Jordan, the Rhone, the Loire and the Tagus
   will deviate
Hunger will be sated by a mule
The fleet scattered, bodies and blood floating on the
   waters.

Perhaps a Muslim invasion of Europe. Libya has previously been accused of sponsoring terrorism – symbolised by the destruction of airliners – and may not always be as quiescent as of late.

De nuict soleil penseront avoir veu,
Quand le pourceau demi-homme on verra
Bruict, chant, bataille, au ciel battre aperceu:
Et bestes brutes à parler lon orra.

They will dream they have seen the sun by night
When the half-man, half-pig appears
Noise, song, battles, combats in the sky
Brute beasts will be heard to speak.

Scientists have already tested great mirrors that can light up the sky from space, turning night into day. The creation of these mirrors eerily coincides with the cloning of animals and of human beings. The pig is now known to be the animal nearest to us in some biological senses and their organs are already being exploited for medicine.

⧗ 2044 ⧗

Le parc enclin grande calamité.
Par l'Hesperie et Insubre fera
Le feu en nef peste et captivité,
Mercure en l'Arc Saturne fenera.

The park, through great calamity, will slope
This will be done throughout the West, and Italy
A fire on board ship, plague and captivity
Mercury in Sagittarius will ruin Saturn.

Hesperie can be taken to mean either the West as a whole, or America. The 'sloping park' implies a vast earthquake, set to take place on 7 December 2044, the year of the next full conjunction of Saturn and Mercury entering Sagittarius.

⧗ 2050 ⧗

Les lieux peuplez seront inhabitables
Pour champs avoir grand division
Regnes livrez à prudents incapables
Lors les grands freres mort et dissention.

Inhabited lands will become uninhabitable
Land will cause division
Power will be given to imprudent men
Death and dissension for the great brothers.

When Nostradamus was writing in the 1550s, the world's population was under 500 million, and the effects of agricultural and industrial revolution had not yet been felt in the world. By the 2050s, global population is projected at 10 billion, with great tracts of the planet beyond either cultivation or settlement.

⏳ 2051 ⏳

Un an devant le conflict Italique
Germains, Gaulois, Hespaignols pour le fort
Cherra l'escolle maison de republique
Ou, hors mis peu, seront suffoque mors.

One year before the Italian war
Germans, French and Spanish will support the strongest
The republic's house of learning will fall
Where all but a few will suffocate to death.

Future conflict in federal Europe – with economic origins. Italy, irredeemably mired in debt, faces partition. The wealthy, productive North proposes separation from the corrupt and aid-dependent South. Germany, France and Spain vote in the federal parliament to recognise a northern-Italian state but other states oppose. In the vacuum, Italy falls into chaos.

Un regne grand demourra desolé
Aupres del Hebro se feront assemblees
Monts Pyrenees le rendront consolé
Lors que dans Mai seront terres tremblees.

A great kingdom is desolated
They will gather near the Ebro
The Pyrenees will console him
For the May earthquakes.

The Ebro is the great river of northeast Spain, defining a one-hundred-mile zone south of the Pyrenees. This quatrain is believed to augur a great disaster in the region, possibly the earthquakes mentioned, but just as likely a politically earth-shaking event connected with, say, Spain's participation in the European federal experiment or Basque nationalism. The month of May has been interpreted as code for the number 5 and thus possibly a prediction of five centuries forward to around 2055.

Selin monarque l'Italie pacifique
Regnes unis Roi chrestien du monde
Mourrant voudra coucher en terre blesique
Apres pirates avoir chassé de l'onde.

With a Selin king, Italy is peaceful
Kingdoms are united by the terrestrial Christian King
When he dies, he will wish to be buried in Blois
Having chased the pirates from the high seas.

Blois in the Loire Valley of France is the seat of the dukes of
Orleans and thus, of the French kings of Nostradamus's own
time. The beautiful château of the Renaissance is still standing.
He visualises this dynasty, symbolised by Selin (from the Greek
for Moon – heraldic device of Henri II) producing a king who will
scatter the pirates (meaning the heathen, as exemplified by north
African corsairs) and unite Europe under a Christian banner. A
happy, if optimistic, prospect for the 500th anniversary of the
untimely death of Henri II.

2062

Durant l'estoille chevelue apparente,
Les trois grans princes seront faits enemis
Frappés du ciel paix terre tremulante,
Pau, Timbre undans, serpent sus le bort mis.

When the bearded star appears
The three princes will argue
The world's fragile peace will be struck at from the skies
And a serpent will be placed on the shores of the
winding Tiber and the Po.

The bearded star is undoubtedly Halley's Comet, which last appeared in 1986. Commonly acknowledged to presage great wars and upsets, the comet's next appearance is due in 2062. Astronomer Edmund Halley (1656–1742) knew he would not live to see the return of the comet whose orbit he had identified – in the first scientific celestial prophecy – but the heavenly apparition duly appeared, precisely as predicted, sixteen years after Halley's death, in 1758.

Apres grand troche humaine plus grand s'appreste,
Le grand moteur des Siecles renouvelle
Pluie, sang, laict, famine, fer et peste,
Au ciel veu feu, courant long estincelle.

Following one misery, a further misery lies in wait
    for mankind
The great cycle of the centuries brings renewal
Rain, blood, milk, hunger, cold steel and plague
Fire will light up the sky, dragging a trail of sparks
    behind it.

This is one of Nostradamus's many foretellings of Armageddon,
to be signposted by the flaming tail of a comet. Halley's Comet,
one of the most frequent visitors, is next due in 2062.

⧗ 2062 ⧗

Mabus puis tost alors mourra, viendra,
De gens et bestes une horrible defaite
Puis tout à coup la vengeance on verra,
Cent, main, soif, faim, quand courra la comete.

Soon Mabus will kill all, then will come
A terrible undoing of animals and people
Then, suddenly, vengeance will appear
In the form of a comet; hunger, thirst, a hundred hands.

Self-destruction awaits us all in a distaster presaged by a comet –
possibly Halley's, next due in 2062. *M'abus* means 'I abuse
myself'.

⧗ 2066 ⧗

Par quarante ans l'Iris n'apparoistra,
Par quarante ans tous les jours sera veu
La terre aride en siccité croistra,
Et grans deluges quand sera apercu.

For forty years no rainbow will appear
For a further forty, it will be seen each day
The arid earth will grow more parched
Then floods, when a rainbow is seen again.

A prediction of apocalyptic climate change in which drought is succeeded by flood – a vision, perhaps, of the long-term consequences of global warming

Flambeau ardent au ciel soir sera veu
Pres de la fin et principe du Rosne
Famine, glaive: tard le secours pourveu
La Perse tourne envahir Macedoine.

A burning flame will appear in the night sky
Near both the source and the estuary of the Rhone
Famine, swords: help will come late
Persia turns and invades Macedonia.

No doubt about the last line. Persia, now Iran, reverses history
by avenging its destruction by the Macedonian giant of history,
Alexander the Great, who burnt Persepolis in a drunken fit in
330BC. Macedonia is now an unstable former republic of the
Yugoslav federation. Nostradamus predicts that the country will
submit itself to the Muslim faith, and that conflicts elsewhere in
Europe will deny aid against the invader.

La gent estrange divisera butins
Saturne et Mars son regard furieux,
Horrible estrange aux Toscans et Latins
Grec qui seront a frapper curieux.

The alien race will divide the spoils
Saturn and Mars will have an angry aspect
Horrible and strange to the Tuscans and Romans
Greeks will wonder whether to strike.

Nostradamus envisions a time when war between nations –
exemplified by Greece and Italy – will be interrupted by the
appearance of a common enemy, an alien race. Perhaps from
another continent, possibly even from a distant world.

2089

Tout aupres d'Auch, de Lectoure et Mirande,
Grande feu du ciel en trois nuits tombera,
Chose adviendra bien stupende et mirande,
Bien peu après al terre tremblera.

All around Auch, Lectoure and Mirande
A great fire will fall from the sky for three nights
A stupendous, marvellous thing will happen
Soon after, the ground will shake.

Nostradamus describes these convulsing events as wonderful
rather than terrifying, so a celestial event rather than an earthly
bombardment is presaged. Auch is a city of southwest France
famed for its immense Gothic cathedral, started in 1489. It
remained staunchly Catholic throughout the religious wars of
the sixteenth century. Perhaps the seer believed it would be a
just reward for the city to witness a great heavenly happening,
when it comes.

Un qui des dieux d'Annibal infernaux
Fera renaistre, effrayeur des humains
Oncq' plus d'horreur ne plus dire journaulx
Qu'avint viendra Babel aux Romains.

One who calls up the infernal gods
Of Hannibal, terror of mankind
Even more horror, more than the papers tell
Then the Romans come, through Babel.

Hannibal (247–183BC) was the Carthaginian soldier who came very close indeed to conquering Rome by marching on Italy through France and across the Alps in 218BC. Nostradamus foresees an imperial invader similarly able to win unexpected victories, who comes through Babel – an allegory for a place of diverse foreign tongues. Alludes to an invasion of Europe from a future Asian superpower.

Du pont Euxine, et la grand Tartarie,
Un roi sera qui viendra voir la Gaule
Transpercera Alane et l'Armenie,
Et dans Bisance lairra sanglante Gaule.

From the Black Sea and great Tartary
A king will come, to France
He will cross Russia and Armenia
And raise his bloody standard in Byzantium.

The third Anti-Christ is due to come from the East. Could he be the new Messiah predicted elsewhere by Nostradamus, or will he be evil, bringing terror to the Earth? The fact that he raises a 'bloody standard' does not bode well.

La voix ouie de l'insolite oiseau,
Sur le canon du respiral estage
Si hault viendra du froment le boisseau,
Que l'homme de l'homme fera Antropophage.

The cry of a strange bird
Will be heard through the chimney shafts
The cost of wheat will rise so high
That men will become cannibals.

Owls, and other avian spiritual messengers, are often accepted as harbingers of doom. Another interpretation could have the words 'strange bird' describing a bomber letting loose its cargo of destruction on those below. Following the nuclear war, the cost of wheat would become so punitive that mankind would revert to cannibalism in an effort to ward off annihilation.

Trop le ciel pleure l'Androgyn procrée,
Pres de ciel sang humain respondu
Par mort trop tard grand peuple recrée,
Tard et tost vient le secours attendu.

The heavens weep too much when the
    Hermaphrodite breeds
High in the sky, human blood is shed
Through death, a great race can no longer
    be recreated
Sooner or later the expected help will come.

This can now be seen as a reference to human cloning, leading to possible warfare later on. Within a century, unprincipled governments will be experimenting, in deepest secret, with the possibilities of genetic morphology. The expected help is likely to be that the Frankenstein-type 'great race' will be the instrument of its own destruction.

A quarante huict degré climaterique
A fin de Cancer si grande seicheresse
Poisson en mer, fleuve, lac cuit hectique
Bearn, Bigorre par feu ciel en destresse.

At the 48th climacteric degree
At the end of July, there will be a great drought
The fish of the sea, rivers and lakes will be boiled
    alive
Bearn and Bigorre will suffer from fire from the sky.

A clear prediction of global warming and its disastrous implications. If forecasts by climatologists are to be believed. World temperatures will increase by as much as three degrees centigrade during the 21st century. That's six times the rise of the 20th century. Extrapolating, the sea will boil well before the fourth millennium of the Christian era.

Un peu de temps les temples de couleurs
De blanc et noir des deux entremeslee
Rouges et jaunes leur embleront les leurs
Sang, terre, peste, faim, feu, d'eau affollee.

Soon the temple of colours
Black and white intermixed
Reds and yellows will take theirs away
Blood, earth, plague, hunger, fire, maddened by
　　　thirst.

A vision of a multi-racial society bound together by the elements of the last line. It suggests that when these boundary-crossing troubles afflict the whole world, as surely they will, we will at last put nationalism aside and live together as one race – with our humanity in common. An optimistic outlook for the third millennium.

⧖ 2100 ⧖

Par la tumeur de Heb, Po, Tag, Timbre et Rome
Et par l'estsange leman et Arentin
Les deux grands chefs et citez de Garonne
Prins mors noyez. Partir humain butin.

Because of the flooding of the Ebro, Po, Tagus, Tiber
   and Rhone
And also of the lakes of Leman and Arezzo
The two main chiefs and their cities of the Garonne
Are taken, dead, drowned. The people divide the booty.

Global warming threatens a substantial rise in sea levels,
through the thermal expansion of the oceans, attended by the
additional risk of major thaw in the polar ice caps, during the
third millennium. One well-supported projection has sea levels
rising five metres by the end of the twenty-first century.

Le prince Arabe Mars, Sol, Venus, Lyon
Regne d'Eglise par mer succombera
Devers la Perse bien pres d'un million
Bisance, Egypte, ver. serp. invadera.

The Arab prince, Mars, the Sun, Venus and Leo
The church's realm will succumb by sea
Nearly a million men will invade Egypt and Byzantium
Followers of the true serpent, from the direction of
    Persia.

Trouble afoot in the Middle East. From the direction of Persia
(Iran) comes an invasion of Turkey and Egypt and the
extinction of Christianity in the region. The incursion would
appear to be doctrinal rather than military.

2126

Pendant que l'aigle et le coq à Savone
Seront unis Mer Levant et Ongrie
L'armee à Naples, Palerne, Marque d'Ancone
Rome, Venise par Barb' horrible crie.

While the cock and the eagle are at Savona
The Eastern and Hungarian seas will be united
The army is at Naples, Palermo, the marches of Ancona
Rome, Venice, great cries from the barbarian.

The cock signifies France, and there is the chance that the eagle
here represents America – forming a western alliance against a
threat from the East. Barbarian can be taken to mean a Muslim
invasion and the route is clearly through the Mediterranean.

Depuis Monach jusque aupres de Sicile
Toute la plage demourra desolée
Il n'y aura fauxbourg, cité ne ville
Que par Barbares pillé soit et volée.

From Monaco, to near Sicily
The entire coast will be desolated
There will be neither suburb, town nor city
That has not been pillaged and robbed by the
    Barbarians.

Nostradamus was known to refer to Muslims as Barbarians. He
foresees a time when Islam invades all of Italy.

 2142

Les deux unis ne tiendront longuement
Et dans treize ans au Barbare Satrappe
Au deux costez seront tel perdement
Qu'un benira le Barque et sa cappe.

The two will not remain united for long
In thirteen years to the Barbarian Satrap
There will be such loss, on both sides
That one man will bless the Papal ship and cape.

The satraps were the provincial governors of the ancient Persian empire. Here a new empire is perceived in decline because an alliance is breaking up. Perhaps an internecine disintegration of relations between Russia and the former client states of the Soviet Union.

2150

De l'aquatique triplicité naistra.
D'un qui fera le jeudi pour sa feste
Son bruit, loz, regne, sa puissance croistra,
Par terre et mer aux Oriens tempeste.

A triumvirate will be born from the water
One of whom will take Thursday for his feast day
His renown, praises, reign and power will grow
Bringing the East unrest, from land and sea.

This is a reference to the Third Antichrist, who will have the water signs of Aries, Cancer and Aquarius dominant in his birth sign. The fact that he will take Thursday for his feast day implies, in Nostradamus's strict dogmatic interpretation of the scriptures, that he will be a pagan being, causing others to worship him.

🏛 2168 🏛

Soleil levant un grand feu l'on verra
Bruit et clarté vers Aquilon tendants
Dedans le rond mort et cris l'on orra
Par glaive, feu, faim, mort las attedants.

A great fire will be seen at sunrise
Its noise and light extending to the North
Death and cries shall be heard in the darkness
Death awaits them through sword, fire and famine.

This is a fire that comes suddenly, an ominous picture of a great explosion presaging not just war, but famine.

Par les contrees du grand fleuve Bethique
Loing d'Ibere au royaume de Grenade
Croix repoussees par gens Mahometiques
Un de Cordube trahira la contrade.

Through the lands either side of the Guadalquivir
Far from Spain, to the kingdom of Granada
The cross is pushed back by the Mahommedans
A Cordoban man will betray his country.

Granada, the last Moorish stronghold in Spain, fell to the armies
of Ferdinand and Isabella, on 2 January 1492. It is one of the
great dates in history – the end of centuries of Mohammedan
influence in Europe. But it marked a bleak time for the Jews in
Spain. Muslim rulers had always been tolerant, but now that the
power of the Catholic Church was absolute, all Jews in the
country – about 150,000 of them – were summarily expelled.
Some of Nostradamus's own forbears were undoubtedly among
them. The seer must have had mixed feelings about this distant
prospect of a Muslim re-invasion of Spain.

⧗ 2193 ⧗

La grand copie qui passera les monts,
Saturne en l'Arq tournant du poisson Mars
Venins caches soubs testes de saulmons,
Leur chef pendu à fil de polemars.

The great army, which crosses the high passes
Saturn in Sagittarius aspects Mars in Pisces
Hidden poison in salmon-heads
Their war chief will be hanged by a cord.

The conjunction of the planets mentioned in the quatrain last
occurred on 7 July 1751. It will occur again on 13 July 2193. Could
the poison hidden in salmon-heads refer to toxins from some
future farmed marine food?

De Fez le regne parviendra à ceux d'Europe
Feu leur cité et lame trenchera
Le grand d'Asie terre et mer à grand troupe
Que bleux, pers, croix, à mort dechassera.

From Fez the kingdom will reach Europe
Their city blazes and the sword slashes
The great Asian leader will cross land and sea with a
   large army
He will drive out and kill the blues, the Persians and
   those of the cross.

Nostradamus visualises a Muslim invasion of Europe from the
Persian Gulf, aided by a power base in north Africa. Not
necessarily a military takeover but quite possibly a doctrinal
ingress as the Christian faith retreats. Some traditions date this
transcending event to the year 2570, the start of the third
Mohammedan millennium.

2769

Saturne en Cancer, Jupiter avec Mars
Dedans Feurier Chaldondon salvaterre
Sault Castalon affailli de trois pars
Pres de Verbiesque conflit mortelle guerre.

Saturn in Cancer, Jupiter with Mars
In February a soothsayer saves the earth
Sierra Morena is besieged on three sides
Near Verbier there is war and mortal conflict.

Astrologers date this event at 1 February 2769. It appears that a
warning about a war will be heeded, and the world saved.

⧗ 2880 ⧗

Lune obscure cie aux profondes tenebres,
Son frère passe de couleur ferrigine;
Le grand cache long temps soubs les tenebres,
Tiendra fer dans la pluie sanguine.

The moon hidden in deep darkness
Her brother changes to a reddish colour
The great one hides for long in darkness
He will wreak destruction in a rain of blood.

The sun the colour of blood; the moon unseen; raining blood. A vision of ultimate destruction in which the world is, quite literally, darkened. An uncomfortable portent of what might follow an asteroid strike of the type astronomers have already predicted for the year 2880 – on the basis of a 300-to-1 risk.

Au lieu que Hieron feit sa nef fabriquer,
Si grand deluge sera et si subite,
Qu'on n'aura lieu ne terres s'atacquer
L'onde monter Fesulan Olympique.

Where Jason built his ship
Will come a great and sudden flood
There will be no land left to cling to
The waves will rise over Mount Olympus.

Another meteor strike prediction, with impact somewhere in the Aegean. Mount Olympus is 9,570 feet above sea level, so the resulting tsunami will be an overwhelming one.

La grand estoille par sept jours brulera,
Nuée fera deux soleils apparoir
Le gros mastin fera toute nuict hurlera,
Quand grand pontife changera de terroir.

The bright star will burn for seven days
The smoke therefrom will cause two suns to appear
All night the great hound will howl
When the pope changes his abode.

Taken by many to refer to the 'double sun' effect of a nuclear explosion, it could just as easily pertain to the aftermath of a meteorite striking the Earth. The hot core of the star might burn for seven days, throwing dense clouds of smoke into the atmosphere from which the sun would reflect, producing, in effect, 'two suns'.

⧗ 3255 ⧗

Beaucoup, beaucoup avant telles menées,
Ceux d'Orient par la vertu Lunaire,
L'An mil sept cens feront grands emmenées,
Subjugant presque le coin Aquilonaire.

Long, long before such events
The people of the Orient by stealth
In 1700 years' time will expel great numbers
Subjugating nearly all the north.

The events referred to in the first lines are the consuming of the earth by the sun and the end of humanity in the year 7000. But before this happens, the Chinese will take over most of the northern hemisphere (Aquile is an old word for the North).

⌛ 7000 ⌛

Vingt ans du regne de la lune passez,
Sept mil ans autre tiendra sa monarchie,
Quand le soleil prendra ses jours laissez,
Lors accomplit a fine ma Prophecie.

After 20 years of the moon's reign
Another monarch will take hold for 7,000 years
When the sun takes the remaining days
Then my prophecy is finally accomplished.

Armageddon: the sun will consume the earth, around the year 7000. In fact, this is not Nostradamus's own prediction. He has adapted it from the pre-Christian Book of Enoch.

⧗ 7000 ⧗

Au revolu du grand nombre septiesme,
Apparoistra au temps jeux d'Hecatombe,
Non esloigné de grand d'age milliesme,
Que les entrez sortiront de leur tombe.

When the great number seven rolls around
Will come the time of games at the Hecatomb
Not far from the great Millennium age
When the interred will depart from their tomb.

In the eighth millennium, the dead will walk. Earth joins with Heaven, or with Hell.

Predictions of Nostradamus for the
20th CENTURY

Un peu devant monarque trucidé
Castor, Pollux en nef, estre crinite
L'erain public par terre et mer vuidé
Pise, Ast, Ferrare, Turin, terre interdicte.

A little before a king is killed
Castor and Pollux on board ship, a comet is seen
The public wealth is emptied, by land and sea
Pisa, Asti, Terrara and Turin are forbidden territory.

A presage of the First World War (1914–18), triggered by the assassination of Archduke Ferdinand in Sarajevo. Halley's comet was seen in the sky in 1910.

Le grand theatre se viendra se redresser
Les des jettez et les rets ja tendus
Trop le premier en glaz viendra lasser
Par ares prostrais de long temps ja fendus.

The great theatre will rise again
The dice are thrown, the nets stretched
The first one to toll the knell will tire too much
Destruction by beams split long ago.

Nostradamus tunes into the future to visualise the age of that limitless theatre, the broadcast. The stretching of the nets and the tolling of the knell suggest performances seen and heard over distances. Wireless telegraphy dates from around 1910.

1912

Au regne grand du grand regne regnant
Par force d'armes les grands portes d'airain
Fera ouvrir le roi et duc joignant,
Port demoli nef à fons jour serain.

In the kingdom of the great one, reigning well
The king and the duke, allied together
Will force the brass gates open, by strength of arms
The hull is destroyed, the ship sunk, the day is serene.

Foretelling the loss of the *Titanic*, the great one is Cronus, chief sibling of the twelve Titans of Greek creation mythology. Together they ruled the universe for aeons until Cronus was dethroned by his son, Zeus. Cronus is the king, Zeus the duke. The *Titanic*, the apparently unsinkable flagship of the British White Star Line, was named in honour of the Titans. Allied together, Zeus and Oceanus, another of the Titans, forced the brass gated bulkheads open and sank the ship. The weather on the night was indeed serene.

1914

Deux revoltes faicte du maling falcigere,
De regne et siecles faict permutation
Le mobil signe à son endroit si ingere,
Aux deux egaux et d'inclination.

Two revolutions will be fomented by the evil
     scythe-bearer
Kingdoms will alter at the turn of the century
Libra moves into its house
And both sides are well balanced.

Saturn is the scythe bearer, and the two revolutions are those of
France in 1789 and Russia in 1917. Libra is the house that governs
Austria, whose Empire foundered following the death of Arch-
duke Ferdinand in 1914. His assassination led directly to the First
World War, in which the two sides were, for most of the war at
least, equally balanced.

⌛ 1914–18 ⌛

Des region subjectes à la Balance
Feront troubler les monts par grand guerre
Captifz tout sexe deu et tout Bisance
Qu'on criera à l'aube terre à terre.

From the Libran regions will come men
To disturb the mountains with a great war
Both sexes will be captured, and all Byzantium
So that cries will be heard at dawn, from land to land.

Libra sometimes signifies Britain in Nostradamian code. If true here, the likely theatre is the Middle East during the First World War of 1914–18, when the Turks (Byzantium) were expelled by Arab forces with the inspirational assistance of T. E. Lawrence (1888–1935) as well as that of the British army commanded by General Allenby which relieved Damascus in October 1918.

1916

Par fureur faincte d'esmotion divine,
Sera la femme du grand fort violee
Juges voulans damner telle doctrine,
Victime au peuple ignorant imolee.

Through the feigned fury of divine emotion
The wife of the great one will be badly wronged
Judges, wishing to condemn such a doctrine
The victim will be sacrificed to the ignorant people.

Grigori Rasputin (1872–1916), the 'mad monk' whose magnetic personality and ability to alleviate the Tsarevich's haemophilia endeared him to Empress Alexandra, Tsar Nicholas II's wife. His power became so great that in 1916 he was assassinated by a group of noblemen.

1917

Gymnique sexe captive par hostage
Viendra de nuit custodes decevoir
Le chef du camp deceu par son langage
Lairra à la gente, sera piteux à voir.

A female prisoner will arrive by night
To deceive the guards
The camp leader, deceived by her tongue
Hands her to his people; it is pitiful to see.

Can Nostradamus have foreseen the short, eventful life and pitiable death of Mata Hari, the Dutch dancer arrested on trumped-up spying charges in Paris in 1917 and shot by firing squad?

Es lieux et temps chair un poisson donra lieu
La loi commune sera faicte au contraire
Vieux tiendra fort plus osté du millieu
Le Pánta chiona philòn mis fort arriere.

When meat gives way to fish
Common law will dictate the opposite
The old order will hold, then be ousted
The Common Order will fall behind.

Meat giving way to fish equates to the contemporary phrase about frying pans and fires. The people of Russia lost their despotic tsar in 1917, only to have his regime replaced with an equally tyrannical communist rule. And as Nostradamus predicts, this new Common Order will fail in its time, as it did in 1990.

1918

O quel horrible et malheureux tourment,
Trois innocens qu'on viendra à livrer
Poison suspecte, mal garde tradiment,
Mis en horreur par bourreaux enivrez.

Three innocent people are subjected
To a most terrible and wretched torture
Poison will be suspected, and treason
In horror they face drunken executioners.

Russian Tsar Nicholas II (1868–1918), his wife Aleksandra, his
son Alexis, and his four daughters, Olga, Tatiana, Marie and
Anastasia, were put to death on 16 July 1918 at Yekaterinburg,
Siberia. The three innocent people mentioned in the quatrain
were, arguably, their physician, Prince Dolgorolkoff, Alexis's
nurse, and the Czarina's lady-in-waiting, who were executed at
the same time as their masters – presumably to stop them from
talking. Their executioners were indeed drunk, on vodka.

Par conflict Roi, regne abandonnera
Le plus grand chef faillira au besoing
Mors profligés peu en rechapera
Tous destranchés un en sera tesmoing.

The king abandons his kingdom because of a battle
The greatest leader will fail when needed
Death, ruination, few will escape
All killed, save one witness.

The fate of Kaiser Wilhelm II, forced to abdicate after Germany's defeat in the First World War. Contrary to the allied propaganda of the time, the Kaiser was not a ferocious warmonger, but the impotent puppet of his generals.

Tard arrivé, l'execution faite
Le vent contrare, lettres au chemin prinses,
Les conjurez quatorze d'une secte,
Par le Rousseau seront les entreprinses.

Arriving late, the execution carried out
The wind against them and letters lost on the way
The beseeching group of fourteen
The Red ones will be their undertakers.

The murder of Tsar Nicholas II of Russia with his family and household by Red Guards on the day they arrived at Yekaterinberg in the Urals on 16 July, 1918. Bolshevik officials in Moscow, wishing to distance themselves from the crime, claimed bad weather and communications had prevented their intervention in a decision taken without consultation by local secret police.

1918

Mont Aventine brusler nuict sera veu
Le ciel obscur tout à un coup en Flandres
Quand le monarque chassera son nepveu
Leurs gens à Eglise commettront les esclandres.

They will see Mount Aventine burning by night
The sudden obscuring of the heavens in Flanders
When the monarch chases out his nephew
Their church people will cause scandals.

The end of the First World War. Kaiser Wilhelm II's forces were
driven out of France and the Low Countries by forces under the
titular control of his blood relation, George V of Great Britain.

Et Ferdinand blonde sera descorte,
Quitter la fleur suivre le Macedon.
Au grand besoin faillira sa routte,
Et marchera contre le Myrmidon.

Fair Ferdinand will lose everything
Leaving the flower to follow Macedonia
In great necessity his course will fail him
He will march against the Myrmidons

King Ferdinand of Bulgaria abandoned his beloved France and sided with Germany during World War I, in the mistaken belief that the Kaiser would help him regain Macedonia. The Kaiser abandoned him in 1918, leaving him to face the French and the Serbs (Myrmidons) alone. Stripped bare by the treaty of Versailles, he fled Bulgaria at the end of the war, to be succeeded by his son, Boris III.

Des innocens le sang de vessue et vierge.
Tant de maulx faitz par moyen se grand Roge
Saintz simulacres tremper en ardent cierge
De frayeur crainte ne verra nul ne boge.

The blood of innocents, widows and virgins
The great Red One commits many evils
Holy images burn in ardent flame
Terrified and fearful, no one will dare to move.

The Russian Revolution of 1919, in which the great Red One was responsible for the destruction of countless Orthodox churches, and the murder of many innocents, which, to Nostradamus's royalist eyes, would include the Tsar and his family.

Premier grand fruit le prince de Perquiere
Mais puis viendra bien et cruel malin
Dedans Venise perdra sa gloire fiere
Et mis à mal par plus joune Celin.

First, the great fruit of the prince of Peschiera
Afterwards will come a cruel and wicked man
In Venice he will lose his proud glory
He is led into evil by the youngest Selin.

The prince of Peschiera is King Victor Emmanuel III of Italy (1869–1947), who brought his country into the First World War against Germany and bravely commanded his army. In 1922, to save Italy from civil war, he offered the premiership to Benito Mussolini and therby effectively lost control of his realm.

1923

Qui ouvrira le monument trouvé
Et ne viendra le serrer promptement.
Mal lui viendra et ne pourra prouvé,
Si mieux doit estre roi Breton ou Normand.

The man who opens the tomb, after its discovery
And does not shut it straight away
Evil will strike him, no one can prove it
He should rather have been a Breton or Norman king.

Howard Carter (1873–1939), a British archaeologist, and his patron, George Herbert, 5th Earl of Carnarvon (1866–1923), discovered the opulent tomb of Tutankhamen, an eighteenth dynasty Egyptian Pharaoh, in 1922. Despite rumours of a curse, they opened the tomb in 1923. It was untouched, and contained the magnificent mummy of the boy-king, together with his immensely valuable funeral relics. Carnarvon died two months later, in Cairo, as the result of an infected mosquito bite he inadvertently cut, while shaving. At exactly the same moment, back in England, his beloved dog also died.

Du hault du mont Aventin voix ouie,
Vuidez, vuidez de tous les deux costez,
Du sang des rouges sera l'ire assomie,
D'Arimin Prate, Columna debotez.

A voice is heard from the Aventine heights
Leave, leave, all of you, on both sides
Anger will only be appeased with the blood of the reds
Colonna is expelled from Rimini and Prato.

Roman senators used to retreat to the Aventine heights when no
further dialogue was possible. In 1924, the Italian socialist
opposition left the Chamber in protest at the murder, by
fascists, of Deputy Matteoti. Mussolini, who was born near
Rimini and Prato, and who, like Colonna, had the Vatican on
his side, used their absence to force through new vote-rigging
tactics.

⌛ 1925 ⌛

La Liberté ne sera recouvrée,
L'occupera noir, fier, vilain, inique,
Quand la matière du pont sera ouvrée,
D'Hister, Venise faschée la république.

Liberty will not be recovered
Power will be held by a proud, villainous,
    iniquitous man
When the matter of the bridge is opened
By Hister at Venice, angering the republic.

Benito Mussolini, dictator of Italy from 1925 to 1943, first met Adolf Hitler in Venice, and began the dialogue that was to cost him his country and his life. The matter of the bridge is very likely the agreement between the Pope (*pont* equates to bridge which equates to pontiff) and Mussolini of 1928. The name Hister is unnervingly close to that of the Führer.

⧗ 1935 ⧗

Dans cité entrer excercit desniee,
Duc entrera par persuasion,
Aux foibles portes clam armee amenee,
Mettront feu, mort de sang effusion.

The army is denied access to the city
The Duc enters by persuasion
The army is led, in secret, to vulnerable gates
They will put the place to fire and sword; blood
    will flow.

'Duc' may once again be taken for 'Duce', the title Benito
Mussolini assumed as fascist head of the Italian State after 1925.
The vulnerable gates would then be those of Makale, the
provincial capital of Ethiopia, which fell to the Duce on 8
November 1935.

L'impotent Prince faché, plaincts et querelles
De rapts et pille, par coqz et par Libiques
Grand est par terre par mer infinies voilles
Seule Italie sera chassont Celtiques.

The powerless Prince is angry, he complains and quarrels
There is rape and pillage, both by the cock and the Libyans
The great one stays on land, at sea, many sails
Only Italy chases out the Celts.

France continues to be troubled by its rebellious territories in north Africa, and now the independence of the last free state on the continent is challenged as Italian fascists invade Abyssinia (Ethiopia), starting their campaign on 3 October by shelling a hospital clearly displaying the Red Cross flag.

⌛ 1936 ⌛

Le gouverneur du regne bien scavant,
Ne consentir voulant au faict Royal
Mellile classe par le contraire vent,
Le remettra à son plus desloyal.

The learned governor of the realm
Not wishing to consent to the royal deed
The fleet of Melilla, through a lee wind
Will return him to his most disloyal subject.

General Francisco Franco (1892–1975) launched his revolt against
the elected Spanish Government from Melilla, a Spanish colony
near Morocco, on 18 July 1936, just five years after King Alfonso
XIII (1886–1941) had abdicated and left the country. Franco was
instrumental in restoring the Bourbon monarchy to Spain,
when he named Prince Juan Carlos, Alfonso's grandson, as his
successor, in 1969.

1936

Du plus profond de l'Occident d'Europe
De pauvres gens un jeune enfant naistra
Qui par sa langue seduira grande troupe,
Son bruit au regne d'Orient plus croistra.

From the deepest part of Western Europe
A baby will be born, to a poor family
He will seduce many by his speeches
His reputation will rise in the Eastern kingdom.

Thanks to the last line, this quatrain applies to Adolf Hitler (1889–1945), and not to Napoleon. Born in Austria, in the small village of Braunau am Inn, Hitler was the son of an impoverished customs official. Renowned for the power of his oratory, which held even his opponents spellbound with horror, Hitler signed a pact with Japan (the Eastern Kingdom) in 1936. Japan later allied itself with Hitler against the Allies during the Second World War.

1936

Pour ne vouloir consentir à divorce,
Qui puis apres sera cogneu indigne,
Le Roi des Isles sera chassé par force
Mis à son lieu que de roi n'aura signe.

For not wishing to approve the divorce
And who, incidentally, shall later be considered
    unworthy
The King of the Islands will be forced out
A man will replace him who never expected to be king.

This could describe the abdication of Edward VIII of England, on 10 December 1936. In love with divorcée Wallis Simpson, Edward (1894–1972) was forced into voluntary exile after their marriage, and was later considered unworthy for his tactless dealings with the Nazis. His diffident brother George succeeded him as George VI (1895–1952), becoming one of England's most popular monarchs and the father of the present Queen.

 1936

De castel Franco sortira l'assemblee
L'ambassadeur non plaisant fera scisme
Ceux de Ribiere seront en la meslee
Et au grand goulphre desnier ont l'entrée.

Franco will bring the army from Castille
The ambassador will complain, causing a schism
Rivera's men will be part of the force
The great man will be denied entry to the gulf.

A famous quatrain mentioning the names of both Francisco Franco (1892–1975) and Primo de Rivera (1870–1930), his fascist precursor. On Rivera's death, his son, José Antonio, created a Falange movement in his father's honour; its members later fought on Franco's side in the Spanish Civil War of 1936–39. In 1936 the Republican government of Spain had exiled Franco to the Canary Islands, denying him entry to the Mediterranean Sea.

⧗ 1936 ⧗

De Bourze ville à la dame Guirlande,
L'on mettra sus par la trahison faicte,
Le grand prelat de leon par Formande,
Faux pellerins et ravisseurs defaicte.

From Burgos to the garlanded lady
People will be downtrodden by treason
Through Formande (Formentara?), the
    grand prelate of Leon
Is undone by ravishers and false pilgrims.

Francisco Franco established his military junta at Burgos in
1936, and from there began his push towards Madrid (the
garlanded lady). Meanwhile Formentara and Ibiza had been
taken by the Republicans, although why Nostradamus takes the
trouble to mention Formentara by name is a mystery, as it is
nothing but a tiny and windswept island, with few inhabitants.

Les Cimbres joints avecques leurs voisins,
Depopuler viendront presque l'Espaigne
Gens amassez, Guienne et Limosins,
Seront en ligue, et leur feront compaigne.

The Cimbrians, together with their neighbours
Will decimate nearly the whole of Spain
The people will gather, Guiennese and Limousins
Allying themselves to their company.

The Cimbrians, an ancient North German tribe, here refer to the German and Italian forces who supported Franco's fascist army during the Spanish Civil War. Six hundred thousand Spaniards and their supporters were killed during the conflict, which lasted from 1936–39, many of them congregating in South West France (Guyenne and Limousin) before crossing the border to fight on the side of the Republicans.

Quand les colomnes de bois grande tremblée,
D'auster conduicte couverte de rubriche,
Tant vuidera dehors une grande assemblée,
Trembler Vienne et le pays d'Austriche.

When the great wooden columns tremble
Correct behaviour as covered by the rubric
Will do so much to drive a great assembly outside
Shaking Vienna and the country of Austria.

A vision of Anschluss Day in Austria, 14 March 1938. Huge crowds greeted Hitler in the streets of Vienna. Peace treaties – the rubrics – forbad union between Germany and Austria but Hitler, and many supporters in Austria, swept these sanctions aside.

🏛 1938 🏛

Foibles galleres seront unies ensemble,
Ennemis faux le plus fort en rampart
Faible assaillies Vratislaue tremble,
Lubecq et Mysne tiendront barbare part.

Weak ships are joined together
False enemies, the strongest holds the rampart
The weak are attacked, Bratislava trembles
Lubeck and Meissen will take the side of the barbarian.

The barbarian is Hitler, drawing together the weak ships of
France and Great Britain in the Munich Pact of 1938, in which
Czechoslovakia is carved up in appeasement, giving Germany
control of the Sudetenland and an excuse to annexe the rest of
Czechoslovakia.

1938

Apres les limes brusler les asiniers
Contraints seront changer habits divers
Les Saturnins bruslez par les meusniers
Hors la plupart qui ne sera convers.

After the penance, the refuges are burned
They will be forced to change into other clothing
Those of Saturn burned by the millers
Excepting the greater part, who will not be converted.

Believed to be a reference to the persecution of German Jews by Nazis, culminating in the terrible night of thuggery, arson and looting of 9 November 1938, known as *Kristallnacht* after the seas of broken glass to be found in the streets from buildings attacked in Jewish quarters of cities throughout the country.

1938

L'honissement puant abhominable
Apres le faict sera felicité,
Grand excusé, pour n'estre favourable,
Qu'à paix Neptune ne sera incité.

The abominable, stinking disgrace
Will be lauded after the fact
The great man will be excused for not being favourable
Let us hope that Neptune cannot be persuaded towards peace.

Neville Chamberlain was British Prime Minister at the time of the Munich Pact of 1938. His instincts were to appease rather than to confront Hitler, and he colluded in allowing Hitler to annexe the Sudetenland region of Czechoslovakia on the understanding Germany would immediately thereafter cease its expansion into Europe. He was welcomed back to Britain as a hero. Nostradamus, in line 4, foresees the dangers of appeasement and sends Great Britain – Neptune – a coded message across nearly four centuries that only Winston Churchill seemed capable of understanding.

⌛ 1939 ⌛

De la partie de Mammer grand Pontife,
Subjugera les confins du Danube
Chassera les croix par fer raffe ne riffe,
Captifz, or, bagues plus de cent mille rubes.

The Pope, speaking for Mother Church
Will subdue the borders of the Danube
By a hooked cross he will cause the true cross to be harried
Captives, gold, rings, more than 100,000 rubies.

An indictment of Pope Pius XII (1876–1958), who refused to condemn or to excommunicate either Hitler or Mussolini, following his election to the Pontificate in 1939. The hooked cross in line 3 is the swastika, under whose symbol the Nazis invaded Poland that same year, harrying the Catholic majority. The last line refers to the millions of Jews who were to lose their lives and worldly possessions partially due to the Pope's intransigence. If he had spoken out earlier, Catholic Italy might have rejected Mussolini at an earlier date.

D'où pensera faire venir famine,
De là viendra le rassasiement
L'oeil de la mer par avare canine
Pour de l'un l'autre donra huile, froment.

From the place where he thinks to bring famine
Will come relief
The eye of the sea, like a greedy dog's
One will give oil, the other, wheat.

One of two quatrains referring to Great Britain's isolation and
blockade by Nazi Germany's submarines during the early stages
of the Second World War. The eye of the sea is the submarine's
periscope, and greedy dogs refers to the wolf-packs, a name used
more than once about the U boats which cruised so effectively
beneath the North Atlantic destroying Allied shipping.

⧗ 1940 ⧗

La republique miserable infelice
Sera vastee de nouveau magistrat
Leur grand amus de l'exile malefice,
Fera Sueve ravir leur grand contracts.

The wretched, unhappy republic
Will be devastated by a new government
Ill will, accumulated in exile
Will cause the Swiss to break their vows.

Unoccupied France was devastated by the Vichy government of Marshal Pétain (1856–1951), who took office in 1940 following the German invasion. In the same year, Charles de Gaulle (1890–1970) escaped to London, where he set up an alternative French National Committee. Switzerland enacted a Banking Secrecy Law in 1934 to protect the accounts of Jews living under Nazi rule. This law was arguably broken, when monies held on behalf of Jewish families murdered during the holocaust were not restored to the descendants of their rightful owners.

Long temps sera sans estre habitée,
Ou Signe et Marne autour vient arrouser
De la Tamise et martiaux tentée,
Decevez les gardes en cuidant repouser.

For a long time no one will inhabit
The place watered by the Seine and the Marne
Attempts by London, and its soldiers
Will deceive the guards into thinking them rebuffed.

This could refer to the Fall of Paris on 14 June 1940, when four-fifths of the population fled, abandoning the city to the invading German troops. The final two lines would then refer to the retreat of Dunkirk, ten days earlier, when Hitler not unreasonably assumed that he had England on the run. On that day 200,000 British troops and 140,000 French troops abandoned French shores, leaving over 30,000 of their companions dead or captured.

Le vieil tribun au point de la trehemide.
Sera pressee captif ne deslivrer,
Le veuil non veuil ne mal parlant timide
Par legitime à ses amis livrer.

The old tribune, on the point of weakening
Will be urged not to release the captive
The old, not old, fearful of speaking evil
In order lawfully to free his friends.

Marshal Pétain, leader of Vichy France, conducted lengthy and futile negotiations with the German high command from 1940 to 1943, concerning the release of over a million French prisoners who were being used by the Nazis as slave labour.

Les exiles deportez dans les isles,
Au changement d'un plus cruel monarque
Seront meurtris: et mis deux les scintiles,
Qui de parler ne seront estez parques.

The exiles deported to the islands
By the advent of an even crueller monarch
Will be murdered; two at a time they will be burnt
Especially those not sparing in their speech.

Commentators hesitate before accepting that this quatrain foretells the holocaust, most notably on account of a mistranslation of *et mis deux les scintiles*. The present translation rectifies this, throwing a new, more sinister light on the quatrain. The concentration camps were certainly islands, cut off from the comforts and laws of ordinary humanity. The ovens at Auschwitz and Dachau are beyond description.

1940

En lieu bien proche non esloigné de Venus,
Les deux plus grans de l'Asie et d'Affrique
Du Rhin et Hister qu'on dira sont venus,
Crys, pleurs à Malte et costé ligustique.

In a nearby place, not far from Venice
The leaders of Africa and Asia
Who are said to have come from Hister, and the Rhine
Will cause weeping and tears in Malta, and the Italian
    coast.

On 27 September 1940, a ten-year military and economic tripartite pact was made between Germany, Italy and Japan, which thereafter became known as the Axis. Adolf Hitler and Benito Mussolini met a week later, in the Brenner Pass, to discuss their future war plans, which included the blanket bombing of the island of Malta. The pact ultimately led to the US Fifth Army landing at Salerno, on 9 September 1943, which triggered the full scale invasion of Italy by the allied forces, in 1944.

L'oiseau royal sur la cité solaire,
Sept mois devant fera nocturne augure
Mur d'Orient cherra tonnerre esclaire,
Sept jours aux portes les ennemis à l'heure.

The royal bird will fly over Paris
Nightly prophecies will occur for seven months
The Eastern borders will fall, in thunder and lightning
In seven days the enemy will be at the gates.

The German eagle (royal bird) flew regularly over Paris during the phony war of December 1939 to April 1940, dropping propaganda leaflets among which were to be found quatrains by Nostradamus apparently prophesying French defeat. Eastern borders refers to the Maginot line, which effectively fell in the seven days of the Blitzkrieg, 5–11 June 1940, laying open the gates of Paris to the German invader.

⧗ 1941 ⧗

Par gent estrange, et Romains lointaine
Leur grand cité apres eaue fort troublée
Fille sans trop different domaine
Prins chef, ferreure n'avoir este riblée.

Because of a foreign people, and far off Romans
Their great city will be damaged by water
A girl from nearby
Is taken by the leader, her bonds still in place.

This has been interpreted by several scholars as a presage of
Japan's attack on the American naval base at Pearl Harbour on
7 December 1941. The far-off Romans is Nostradamian for a
distant imperial power. The captive girl may refer to the Pacific
nations invaded by Japan.

⧗ 1942 ⧗

En cité obsesse aux murs hommes et femmes,
Ennemis hors le chef prest à soi rendre
Vent sera fort encontre les gendarmes,
Chassez seront par chaux, poussiere, et cendre.

Both men and women man the walls of the
    besieged city
The enemy, though not their leader, are prepared
    to surrender
A strong wind will delay the constables
They will be driven off by lime, dust and cinders.

This relates to the 160-day siege of Stalingrad, begun on 20 August 1942, in which both Russian men and women manned the desperate defensive lines against Adolf Hitler's army. The Germans only raised the siege after losing 300,000 of their men. The combined Russian losses totalled nearly a million.

Roy trouvera ce qu'il désiroit tant,
Quand le Prelat sera repris à tort,
Response au Duc le rendra mal content,
Qui dans Milan mettra plusieurs à mort.

The King will find what he has desired so much
When the Prelate is wrongfully seized
The Duke's response will make him unhappy
Who in Milan will put several to death.

The Duke is Il Duce, Mussolini. When he was arrested by his German ally in 1943, Italy's king, Victor Emmanuel III, had what he wanted – an end to the fascist regime and the opportunity to change sides in the war.

1943

Naples, Palerme, Sicille, Syracuses
Nouveau tyrans, fulgures feux celestes
Force de Londres, Gand, Bruxelles, et Suses
Grand hecatombe, triomphe faire festes.

Naples, Palermo, Sicily and Syracuse
New tyrants, exploding fire in the sky
An army from London, Ghent, Brussels and Susa
A great slaughter, triumph is fêted.

The Allied landings on Sicily and the Italian mainland, August 1943. Italy had a new tyrant in the shape of Germany after the fall of Mussolini a month earlier. British and Allied troops were wildly fêted as they entered cities such as Palermo and Naples.

1943

A l'ennemy l'ennemy foi promise
Ne se tiendre les captifs retenus
Prins preme mort et le rest en chemise,
Damné le reste pour estre soustenus.

The enemy make a promise to their enemy
It isn't kept, the captives aren't released
One is captured, near death, the rest in their shirts
The rest are damned for sustaining them.

The Vichy Regime in France beautifully fits the image of an enemy making a promise to an enemy. The promise, of course, wasn't kept, and Vichy leader Marshal Pétain (1856–1951) found himself facing trial for treason after the war. Near death refers to the sentence of death passed on him by the court, which was then commuted to life imprisonment. The captives may refer to the thousands of Jews who were rounded up by the notorious Vichy Milice and delivered willingly to the Germans.

Que peste et glaive n'a sceu definer
Mort dans le puis sommet du ciel frappé
L'abbé mourra quand verra ruiner
Ceux du naufrage l'esceuil voulant grapper.

Having survived both plague and sword
He dies in the mountains, struck from the sky
The priest will die when he sees the ruin
Of the lost ones, as they try to climb the ladders.

Nostradamus knew Italy well, and will certainly have visited Monte Cassino, midway between Naples and Rome, where a monastery was first established by St Benedict in the sixth century. The beautiful buildings Nostradamus knew were relentlessly shelled and bombed by the Allies in their advance on Rome in 1944.

⧗ 1944 ⧗

Ce qui vivra and n'aura aucen sens,
Viendra le fer à mort son artifice,
Autun, Chalons, Langres, les deux Sens,
La guerre et la glasse fera grand malefice.

He who lives on will lack direction
His invention will be the weapon of death
Autun, Chalons, Langres will go both ways
War and the death knell will do great harm.

Adolf Hitler survived an assassination attempt in 1944 at the time he was unleashing the first flying bombs against Britain in a desperate, directionless bid to reverse the fortunes of the war. These terrible weapons were the precursors of the intercontinental ballistic missiles of the modern era.

Longtemps au ciel sera veu gris oiseau,
Aupres de Dole et de Touscane terre
Tenant au bec un verdoyant rameau,
Mourra tost grand et finera la guerre.

For some time a grey bird will be seen
In the skies above Dôle and Tuscany
In its beak will be a flowering branch
But the chief will soon die and the war will end.

The grey bird is a traditionally grey-painted Nazi warplane, seen constantly over Italy following the fall of Mussolini. Dorniers, in particular, had cannons in their nose sections, vividly illustrated by Nostradamus's image of a grey bird with a flowering branch in its beak. Hitler, of course, committed suicide in 1945, directly leading to the cessation of hostilities by the Germans.

⧗ 1945 ⧗

Le nouveau faict conduira l'exercite,
Proche apamé jusques au pres de rivage,
Tendant secour de Milannoile eslite,
Duc yeux privé à Milan fer de cage.

A new general will command the army
Soon to be cut off near the river bank
Help will be offered by the Milanese élite
The Duc will be sightless in Milan; an iron cage.

The first two lines detail the final days of the Third Reich, when
Hitler was replacing his Generals with astonishing regularity.
The Milanese turned violently against Mussolini in 1945,
culminating in his murder by communist partisans. The
sightless dead bodies of the Duce, Mussolini, and his mistress,
Clara Petacci, were later strung upside down on the iron cage of
a burnt-out petrol station, and abused by the crowd.

⧗ 1945 ⧗

Pour la faveur que la cité fera,
Au grand qui tost prendra camp de bataille,
Puis le rang Pau Thesin versera
De sang, feux mors noyés de coup de taille.

Because of the favour shown by the city
To the great man, soon to fail on the battlefield
The rank and file will flee, overflowing the Po and
   the Tessin
Much blood and fire, the fallen drowned and cut
   by sabres.

In 1945, the Italians were driven back across the Po and the Ticino rivers by the Allies during their attack on the Fascist Republic at Salò. Benito Mussolini, their leader, and his mistress, Clara Petacci, later had their bodies paraded and abused before an angry crowd in Milan.

Bestes farouches de faim fleuves tranner,
Plus part du champ encontre Hister sera.
En caige de fer le grand fera treisner,
Quand rien enfant de Germain observera.

Beasts, insane with hunger, will cross the river
Most of the field will be against Hister
The great leader will be paraded in a cage of iron
While the German child sees nothing.

A famed quatrain linking the words Hister (Hitler), and German. Joseph Goebbels, Hitler's propaganda minister, had the Nostradamus quatrains brought to his attention by his wife, and made full use of them. He little knew that Hitler's ally, Benito Mussolini would have his body paraded in an iron cage – the charred frame of a fire-bombed petrol station – and that the world would pass judgement on German children for the very fact that they did, indeed, see nothing. Beasts, in line one, refers to the Russian army, which crossed the Elbe.

Du Lac Lemans les sermons fasceront,
Des jours seront reduit par des sepmains,
Puis mois, puis an, puis tous dafaliront,
Les Magistrats damneront leurs loix vaines.

Lake Leman's sermons will cause anger
Days will turn into weeks
Then into months and years, then fail
The lawmakers will damn their empty laws.

A clear vision of the tragic failure of the League of Nations, which was set up in 1920 at Geneva (archaically called Lake Leman) in hope of preventing any further outbreaks of world war. The League was superseded by the United Nations after the Second World War.

⏳ 1945 ⏳

La grand cité sera bien desolee,
Des habitans un seul n'y demoura
Mur, sexe, temple et vierge violee,
Par fer, feu, peste, canon peuple mourra.

The fine city will be desolated
Not a single inhabitant will remain
Walls, sexes, temples and virgins violated
The people will die from cannon, plague,
    sword and fire.

Berlin was sacked by Russian troops in April 1945, during which
mass rapes are known to have taken place. In the course of the
battle nearly a million people lost their lives. Berlin was virtually
obliterated from the map, having already been pounded for
many months by non-stop Allied bombardments in an effort to
demoralise the population.

⌛ 1948 ⌛

Nouvelle loi terre neufve occuper,
Vers la Syrie, Judee et Palestine
Le grand empire barbare corruer,
Avant que Phoebus son siecle determine.

A new land will be occupied by a new law
Towards Syria, Judea and Palestine
The great barbarian empire will decay
Before the sun ends its century.

This relates to the foundation of the new State of Israel, on 14 May 1948. The implication is that the Arab empire will decay before the end of the twentieth century (the century of the sun). According to the Jewish lunar calendar, 1997 was the true end of the millennium.

⌛ 1952 ⌛

Paix, union sera et changement
Estatz, offices bas hault, et hault bien bas
Dresser voyage le fruict premier torment
Guerre cesser, civil proces debatz.

There will be peace, union and change
Estates and offices that were once high, fall, and
    vice versa
The eldest child is tormented by the preparations
    for a voyage
The war ceases amidst legal process and debate.

This is a remarkably astute prediction for the future of Great
Britain after the Second World War, and the steady break-up of
the British Empire. Queen Elizabeth II is the eldest child, and
the voyage is the funeral of her beloved father, George V,
following his death in 1952. During the early course of her reign
over forty colonies were to become independent, and many
ancient offices overturned.

Profonde argile blanche nourrit rocher,
Qui d'un abysme istra l'acticineuse
En vain troublez ne le seront toucher,
Ignorant être au fond terre argileuse.

A white clay from the deep nourishes the rock
Which will bring actinium from an abyss
No one will want to touch it
Being ignorant of the clay in the earth's heart.

Actinium is a radioactive metal (atomic number 89). A clear prediction of mining for radioactive materials and the development of atomic power – with the fears of contamination that attend it.

1956

Dedans l'entrée de Garonne et Baise
Et la forest non loing de Damazan
Du marsaves gelees, puis gresle et bize
Dordonnois gelle par erreur de mezan.

At the entrance to the Garonne and Baise
And the forest, not far from Damazan
Frozen discoveries made at sea, then hail and
    northerly winds
Frost in the Dordogne, but in the wrong month.

Climate change, a regular Nostradamian theme. Some interpreters believe this refers to the uniquely freakish late frosts that struck France in 1956.

⧗ 1956 ⧗

Par vie et mort changé regne d'Ongrie
La loi sera plus aspre que service
Leur grand cité d'hurlements plaincts et crie
Castor et Pollux ennemis dans la lice.

Through life and death the rule of Hungary is changed
Law becomes harsher than servitude
Their great city howls and laments
Castor and Pollux confront each other in the lists.

On 5 November 1956, Hungary's anti-communist revolution
was crushed under the tracks of Soviet tanks.

☒ 1962 ☒

Le chef de Londres par regne l'Americh,
L'isle de l'Escosse tempiera par gellee
Roi Reb auront un si faux antechrist
Que les mettra trestous dans la meslee.

London's leader, through the rule of America
Will burden the Scottish island with an ice cold thing
King Reb will have so false an Antichrist
That they will all be brought into conflict.

Harold Macmillan (1894–1986), Prime Minister from 1957 to
1963 and a friend of the United States, was instrumental in
having the first ice cold Polaris missiles stationed in Scotland
during the late 1950s. The yiddish word *Reb*, in line 3, is a term of
respect for a man, and stems from the Hebrew word *Rabbi*. In
this context it implies that a respected leader may have his
judgement impaired by a false mentor. This leads us to John F
Kennedy and the Cuban Missile Crisis of 1962, which may have
been triggered by a misconceived CIA/Mafia assassination plan
to kill Fidel Castro.

⧗ 1963 ⧗

La mort subite du premier personnage.
Aura changé et mis un autre au regne
Tost, tard venu à si haut et bas aage,
Que terre et mer faudre que on la craigne.

The sudden death of the leading man
Will cause change, making another man leader
Soon, but too late, the young man will attain high office
By land and sea he will be feared.

John F Kennedy (1917–63) was, at just 43 years old, the youngest ever elected President of the United States. When he was assassinated, in Dallas, on 22 November 1963, he was succeeded by Vice President Lyndon Johnson (1908–73). Kennedy had shown his mettle during the Cuban missile crisis of 1962, but his untimely death nipped his longer-term potential in the bud.

Par le trespas du tres vieillart pontif,
Sera esleu Romain de bon aage
Qu'il sera dict que la siege debisse,
Et long tiendra et de picquant ouvrage.

On the death of the aged Pope
A Roman, in the prime of life, will be elected
He will be accused of weakening the Pontificate
He will last long, and cause great damage.

When Pope John XXIII died, in 1963, he was replaced by another Roman Pope, Paul VI, who reigned until 1978. Achieving much, he was nevertheless criticised for his conservative policies, and for allowing Michele Sindona, a Sicilian banker with Mafia links, to take over advising the Vatican Bank. This caused great and lasting damage to the Church, culminating in the financial scandals of the 1980s.

1963

Quatre ans le siege quelque bien peu tiendra,
Un surviendra libidineux de vie
Ravenne et Pise, Veronne soustiendront,
Pour eslever la croix de Pape envie.

The seat will be held, to some good purpose, for four
    years
A sensuous man will take it over
Ravenna, Pisa and Verona will support him
Wishing to raise the Papal cross.

Pope John XXIII (1881–1963) reigned for a little over four years, and presided over the Second Vatican Council which began the process of modernising the Catholic Church. He was replaced by Pope Paul VI (1897–1978), a more worldly, sensuous man, who was at one time reputed to have had a homosexual lover.

1966

Ne bien ne mal par bataille terrestre
Ne parviendra aux confins de Perousse
Rebeller Pise, Florence voir mal estre
Roi nuict blessé sur mulet à noire house.

Neither good nor evil, by earthly battle
Will come to the borders of Perugia
Pisa will rebel, Florence will be hard struck
The King, on a mule, is injured under cover of night.

Earthly battle speaks not of war but of the struggle against the elements. Flooding springs to mind. The floods which struck Florence in 1966 were the worst for seven hundred years. Many priceless paintings, including great Renaissance religious works (no doubt including depictions of Christ's Palm Sunday entry into Jerusalem) were damaged or destroyed.

⧗ 1967 ⧗

Six jours l'assaut devant cité donné
Livree sera forte et aspre bataille
Trois la rendront et à eux pardonné
Le reste à feu et sang tranche traille.

The city is besieged for six days
It is handed over after a long and bitter fight
Three surrender it, and they are pardoned
For the rest fire, bloody slashing and slaughter.

The city is Jerusalem and the siege the Six-Day-War of 5–10 June 1967, in which Israel was victorious over an alliance of Arab states. Of course Jerusalem was not surrendered in military terms, but a process was begun in which, one day, peace between Jews and Palestinians may break out. In the meantime, the killing continues.

⧗ 1967 ⧗

Le vieux monarque dechassé de son regne
Aux Orients son secours ira querre
Pour peur des croix ployera son enseigne
En Mitylene ira par port et par terre.

The old king, chased from his realm
Will go to seek help from the Orientals
Fearing the crosses, he will fold up his banner
Travelling to Mitylene by port and by land.

Said to refer to the seizure of power by a military junta in Greece
in 1967. The reigning monarch, King Constantine (born 1940)
was formally deposed in 1973 and sought help for a return to
power from many sources. Resumption of democracy in Greece
has not been attended by a restoration of the monarchy.

1967

Seront ouys au ceil les armes battre
Celuy an mesme les divins ennemis,
Voudront Loix Sainctes injustement debatre,
Par foudre et guerre bien croyants a mort mis.

Weapons of war will be heard in the sky
The same year will make holy men enemies
They will unjustly suppress Sacred Law
True believers will be put to death.

Holy war, and battles in the skies. The prediction of combat in the air is uncanny. In the light of Nostradamus's Jewish ancestry, can he be anticipating the Arab-Israeli wars from 1967 in which air power has played such a decisive role? A conflict between two states dominated by religious leaders is certainly indicated. Leaders who are prepared to set aside the teachings of their own holy laws in the quest for victory. Leaders who consider the massacre of innocents – true believers – an acceptable price.

⧗ 1968 ⧗

Le successeur vengera son beau frere,
Occupera regne souz umbre de vengeance,
Occis ostacle son sang mort vitupere,
Long temps Bretaigne tiendra avec la France.

The successor will avenge his handsome brother
He will occupy the realm under shadow of vengeance
The obstacle slain, his dead blood seethes in anger
Britain and France will hold together for a long time.

Robert Kennedy (1925–1968) almost had it within his power to
avenge his 'handsome brother' John F Kennedy's 1963 assassination, when he agreed to campaign as Democratic candidate for
the Presidency against Richard Nixon. The CIA has always
privately accepted that JFK was killed by the Mafia, and the
younger Kennedy had made it an article of faith to curtail the
power of organised crime in the US. He was assassinated, before
he could fulfil his pledge, on 5 June 1968, in a Los Angeles hotel.

🟐 1969 🟐

Dedans le coing de Luna viendra rendre,
Ou sera prins and mis en terre étrange.
Les fruits immeurs seront à grand esclandre,
Grand vitupère a l'un grande louange.

Within, he will bring himself to the corner of the moon
Where he will be taken out and put into a strange land
The fruits of the endeavour will be as a great stairway
From great mockery to great praise.

A clear prediction of man's flight within a machine to the moon,
and Neil Armstrong's first steps on its surface on 21 July 1979.
Nostradamus foresees that this endeavour will meet with a
mixed reception back on Earth.

⧗ 1969 ⧗

Par toute Asie grande proscription
Mesme en Mysie, Lysie, et Pamphyilie
Sang versera par absolution
D'un jeune noir rempli de felonnie.

Orders will travel throughout Asia
Reaching even Mysia, Lycia and Pamphilia
Blood will flow in absolution
Because of a young and evil black man.

Muammar Gadaffi was only twenty-seven when he overthrew the regime of King Idris of Libya in 1969 and promoted himself to the highest rank in the revolutionary army – Colonel. Gadaffi has since been a principal perpetrator of what is now called state-sponsored terrorism, causing outrages throughout the world.

⧗ 1974 ⧗

En ce temps là sera frustree Cypres,
De son secours de ceux de mer Egee
Vieux trucidez, mais par mesles et lyphres
Seduict leur Roy, Royne plus outragee.

Cyprus, at that time, will be deprived
Of aid by those from the Aegean sea
The old will die, by cannon and grief
Their king will be seduced, their queen further outraged.

On 15 July 1974 Greek Cypriot troops overthrew the government
of Archbishop Makarios (1913–1977) on the island of Cyprus.
Five days later the Turks invaded the island, vowing to restore
Makarios. They've been there ever since. In the same year, the
Greek monarchy was formally abolished. Makarios was never
reinstated.

1978

Pol mensolee mourra trois lieus du Rosne
Fuis les deux prochains tarasc destrois
Car Mars fera le plus horrible trosne
De coq et d'aigle de France, freres trois.

Celibate Paul will die three leagues from Rome
The next two flee the oppressive Tarascon
Because Mars will reign horribly
Three brothers, from the cock and eagle of France.

Pope Paul VI, the first pontiff to take the name since Paul V (1552–1621), was elected in 1963. He died in 1978 in the Vatican – but had been the most widely travelled pope in history. Paul VI's election fell in the same year as the assassination of President John Kennedy (of the three brothers – acknowledged to be John, Robert and Edward Kennedy) and the horrible reign of Mars concerns the wars in Southeast Asia in which France and then the United States were so destructively embroiled.

⧖ 1978 ⧖

Esleu en Pape, d'esleu sera mocqué
Subit soudain esmeu prompt et timide
Par trop bon doulz à mourir provocqué
Crainte estainte la nuit de sa mort guide.

Elected Pope, he will be mocked by his electors
All of a sudden moved, prompt and timid
He meets his end through being too good
He will fear the death of his guide, on the night he dies.

Son of a glass-blower from Murano, Albino Luciani was elected Pope number 263 in 1978. Taking the name John Paul I, he vowed to reform the existing Catholic bureaucracy, and, in particular, the notorious Vatican Bank. But 34 days after his election, on the very eve of the morning on which he was going to publish his proposals, he was found dead in his bed, with the papers delineating the radical changes he intended to make scattered all about him. The papers were later misplaced.

⌛ 1979 ⌛

Le chef de Perse remplira grande Olchade
Classe Frireme contre gent Mahometique
De Parthe, et Mede, et piller les Cyclades
Repos long temps aux grand port Ionique.

The Persian leader will replenish merchant ships
A trireme fleet will confront the Mahommedans
He will pillage the Cyclades from Parthia and Medea
There will be a long wait in the main Ionian port.

War and the interruption of trade in the Middle East. The
Persian leader is Ayatollah Ruhollah Khomeini (1900–89) who
returned from exile in 1979 after the collapse of the previous
regime. Khomeini declared holy war on America and the West
as well as waging a long conflict with his neighbour Iraq,
causing economic chaos and killing a million Iranian and Iraqi
combatants.

⧗ 1980 ⧗

La grand band et secte crucigere
Se dressera en Mesopotamie
Du proche fleuve compagnie legiere
Que telle loi tiendra pour ennemie.

The numerous followers of the sect of the cross
Will mass in Mesopotamia
A lighter company, from a nearby river
Will find this law inimical.

Mesopotamia, site of the first cities in civilisation, built on the shores of the rivers Tigris and Euphrates, is now divided between modern Iran and Iraq, two of the most belligerent Muslim powers, divided both internally and externally by the laws of religious doctrine. The two nations fought a bitter and inconclusive war from 1980–88, in which a million lost their lives.

⏳ 1980s ⏳

Quand dans poisson fer et lettre enfermée
Hors sortira qui pis fera la guerre
Aura par mer sa classe bien ramée,
Apparoissant près de Latin terre.

When in an iron fish with a letter enclosed
The man who can make war goes out
To sea with a well-equipped fleet
Appearing by the Latin land.

A thoroughly convincing vision of the submarines of the twentieth century, and in particular of the boats now beneath the seas, bearing their orders (letter enclosed) for mass destruction in the event of hostilities. Trident submarines operated by both the United States and the United Kingdom are perpetually on patrol.

1981

Un grand Roi prins entre les mains d'un Joine,
Non loing de Pasque confusion coup coultre
Perpet. Captifs temps que fouldre en la husne,
Lorsque trois freres se blesseront et meutre.

A great king in the hands of a stripling
Near Easter there will be confusion, and the cut of a
    knife
Time's captives, other times when lightning is on top
In an era when three brothers are wounded and killed.

US President Ronald Reagan was shot by a stripling, William
Hinkley Jr, on 30 March 1981. Only surgery (the cut of a knife)
could save him. This was indeed an era of assassinations. The
two Kennedy brothers, Robert and John, had both been killed by
gunmen, and Edward Kennedy, the third brother, probably only
avoided a similar fate by prohibiting himself from high office by
his behaviour at Chappaquiddick, 19 July 1969, when he failed to
report the death, by drowning, of his date, Mary Jo Kopechne.

⧖ 1985 ⧖

Subite joie en subite tristesse
Sera à Romme aux graces embrassees
Deuil, cris, pleurs, larm. sang excellent liesse
Contraires bandes surprinses et troussees.

Sudden joy becomes sudden sadness
This will be at Rome, kissed with grace
Mourning, cries, tears, weeping, good blood mocked
Opposing groups surprised and trussed up.

During 1985 a number of terrorist atrocities occurred near Rome, including bombings, grenade attacks, the hijacking of a TWA airliner on a flight from Athens to Rome, and the attack on Rome airport itself on 27 December, when more than a dozen people were killed, including some of the terrorists.

Si grand famine par une pestifère,
Par pluye longue le long du Pole Artique;
Samarobyn cent lieux de l'hemisphere,
Vivront sans loy, exempt de politique.

Such a great famine and plague
Will rain down the length of the North Pole;
Samarobyn a hundred leagues from the hemisphere
Will live beyond the law or politics.

The clue is in the name Samarobyn, which is clearly Russian – though not in any gazetteer. The allusion fits uncomfortably with the nuclear disaster at Chernobyl in the Ukraine on 25 April 1986. Agricultural land for hundreds of miles around the destroyed reactor remains contaminated and radiation sickness has killed uncountable numbers. The explosion sent radioactive material into the upper atmosphere and the cloud spread over most of the northern hemisphere.

1989

Vers Aquilon grans efforts par hommasse
Presque l'Europe et l'univers vexer,
Les deux eclipses mettra en tel chasse,
Et aux Pannons vie et mort renforcer.

The iron woman will exert herself to the North
Nearly all of Europe and the world is harassed
She will rout the two failed leaders
Life and death will strengthen Hungary.

The mere mention of an Iron Woman is enough to conjure up images of UK Prime Minister Margaret Thatcher, whose joint efforts with US President Ronald Reagan resulted in the cessation of the Cold War in 1989–90, and the temporary side-lining of the European Community. Hungary, which had suffered bitterly under the Russians during the 1956 uprising, finally became an independent state. The two failed leaders could apply to General Galtieri, of Argentina, and to Mikhail Gorbachev of the Soviet Union.

Sur le combat des grans cheveux, legiers
On criera le grand croissant confond
De nuict tuer monts, habits de bergiers
Abismes rouges dans le fossé profond.

Because of the fighting of the mighty light-haired ones
It will be claimed that the great crescent is confounded
At night, on the mountains, those dressed as shepherds
    will kill
There will be red gulleys in the deep ditches.

The great crescent might equally symbolise the sickle insignium of the former Soviet Union or that of Islam. Any claims that the sickle has been confounded certainly came true with the demise of the USSR in 1990 – a collapse of empire significantly accelerated, it should be said, by Soviet humiliation at the hands of Muslim warriors in Afghanistan.

⧗ 1990s ⧗

Conflict barbare, en la cornere noire,
Sang espandu trembler la Dalmatie,
Grand Ismael mettra son promontoire
Rangs trembler secours Lusitanie.

A barbaric conflict in the black horn
Blood will be shed, shaking Dalmatia
Great Ishmael will make inroads
Shaking the ranks of Portuguese rescuers.

Dalmatia – Jugoslavia – is the clue. Nostradamus foresees the bitter conflict involving Muslims (Ishmael was regarded by Muhammad as the ancestor of the Arabs) in the Balkans. The seemingly irrelevant Portuguese represent peacekeeping UN forces.

Il entrera vilain, mechant, infame
Tyrannisant la Mesopotamie,
Tous amis fait d'adulterine d'ame,
Terre horrible, noir de phisonomie.

He will enter, wicked, bad, evil
Tyrannising Mesopotamia
The adulterous lady needs many friends
The land is horrible, and black of aspect

When Saddam Hussein retreated from Kuwait, he had the oil wells set afire, leaving the Persian Gulf under dense, black clouds. The theme was reprised in the conflict of 2003, when wells were again set on fire and trenches filled with burning oil were used to create black smoke to obscure bombing targets. The adulterous lady (the Statue of Liberty, representing the US) may have needed many friends, but had few.

Laict, sang grenouilles escoudre en Dalmatie
Conflict donné, peste pres de Balennes
Cri sera grand par toute Esclavonie
Lors naistra monstre pres et dedans Ravenne.

Milk and the blood of frogs is hatched in Dalmatia
War, pestilence near Balennes
Great will be the cry throughout enslaved Slovenia
When a monster is born in and near Ravenna.

A dark presage of the tragic events in the Balkans in the 1990s. The identity of the monster born both in and near Ravenna is an unsolved enigma. Ravenna is an Italian city and episcopal see much used in Nostradamian allegory. Could it be a code for Pozarevac in Serbia, birthplace in 1941 of one of the great monsters of the century, Slobodan Milosevic?

Le tant d'argent de Diane et Mercure
Les simulacres au lac seront trouvez,
Le figulier cherchant argille neufve
Lui et les siens d'or seront abbrevez.

Despite all the silver of Diana and Mercury
Their images will be found on the lake
For the sculptor looking for new clay
He and his people will be flooded with gold.

A prediction of the death of Diana, Princess of Wales, and of her lover, Dodi Fayed, as well as Diana's final resting place on a lake island on her brother Earl Spencer's Althorp estate. Mercury was the god of trading and commerce, referring to Fayed's mercantile descent.

Cinq et quarante degrés ciel bruslera,
Feu approcher de la grand cité neufve,
Instant grand flamme esparse sautera,
Quand on voudra des Normans faire preuve.

The sky will burn at 45 degrees
Fire approaches the great new city
Immediately a huge and scattered flame leaps up
When they want proof from the Northerners.

The only major city on a 45° latitude is 'New' Belgrade in former Yugoslavia, Serbian capital city for nine hundred years. Nostradamus describes the Nato bombing which began in March 1999, burning the embattled city. The Northerners are of course Nato, the North Atlantic Treaty Organisation.

Nay souz les umbres et journée nocturne
Sera en rege et bonté souveraine
Fera renaistre son sang de l'antique urne,
Renouvellant siecle d'or pour l'aerain.

Born on the day of an eclipse, in the shadows
He will be supreme in rule and goodness
He will renew his blood in the ancient urn
Causing the golden age to turn to brass.

An important quatrain, relating to the eclipse of 11 August 1999. On that day a new saviour will be born, at the exact moment in which the sun is blotted from view. He will lead the world towards a new, more spiritual path, exemplified by the changing of the gold of the twentieth century into the brass of the Aquarian age. The great urn refers to the wisdom of the Greeks, implying that this new messiah will tend towards the rational rather than the superstitious.

Predictions of Nostradamus for the
19th CENTURY

Apres le Roi du saucq guerres parlant
L'isle Harmotique le tiendra à mespris
Quelque ans bous rongeant un et pillant
Par tyrranie à l'isle changeant pris.

After the king of markets speaks of war
The united island despises him
Several good years of plundering and pillaging
The island changes because of tyranny.

The united island would appear to be Great Britain, although the final coming together only took place following the Act Of Union with Northern Ireland in 1800. Wales had already joined England in 1536, and Scotland in 1707. Fortunately, few instances of real tyranny can be found in Britain during the 19th and the twentieth centuries, due to the purely constitutional role of the Monarch.

Le feu estaint, les vierges trahiront
La plus grand part de la bande nouvelle
Fouldre à fer, lance les seulz Roi garderont
Etrusque et Corse, de nuict gorge allumelle.

When the fire is extinguished, raw recruits will betray
The greater part of the new army
Steel lightning, only lances will guard the king
Tuscany and Corsica; throats slit by night.

Inexperienced Italian soldiers will offer scant resistance to
France's forces during the Napoleonic wars.

1800

Le conducteur de l'armée Françoise,
Cuidant perdre le principal phalange
Par sus pave de l'avaigne et d'ardoise,
Soi parfondra par Gennes gent estrange.

The commander of the French army
Fearing the loss of his main force
On the pavement of oats and slate
A foreign race will be undermined through Genoa.

Napoleon sacrificed Massena's starving garrison of 15,000 men at Genoa, on 4 June 1800, to gain a brief respite for his main army before the Battle of Marengo, 14 June, in which he unequivocally defeated the Austrians under Baron von Melas.

Dedans Boulogne voudra laver ses fautes;
Il ne pourra au temple du soleil.
Il volera faisant choses si hautes,
Qu'en hierarchie n'en fut onc un pareil.

In Boulogne he will wish to expiate his failings
He will not be allowed in the temple of the sun
His achievements will be so great
That none of any hierarchy can be his equal.

Napoleon determined to invade England from Boulogne, but Nostradamus considers that for all the great man's achievements, he'll never make it.

1804

De soldat simple parviendra en empire,
De robbe courte parviendra à la longue:
Vaillant aux armes, en Eglise, ou plus pyre,
Vexer les prestres comme l'eau fait l'espagne.

From simple soldier he progressed to Empire
From the short robe he progressed to the long
Valiant in arms, more of a scourge to the Church
Wringing out the priests like water from a sponge.

Napoleon Bonaparte crowned himself Emperor on 2 December 1804, exchanging the modest attire of First Consul for the orotund Imperial regalia. Pope Pius VII was in attendance, but the honour of placing the crowns on the heads of Napoleon and the Empress Josephine was accorded not to His Holiness, but to the Emperor himself. This was symptomatic of the esteem in which Bonaparte held the Church. Five years later, the French annexed the Papal estates, and Pope Pius was arrested.

⌛ 1804 ⌛

Nepveu et sang du sainct nouveau venu
Par le surnom soustient arcs et couvert
Seront chassez mis à mort chassez nu
En ruge et noir convertiront leur vert.

Blood nephew of the newly-created saint
His surname will uphold the arches and the roof
Naked, they will be chased and put to death
Their green will be converted to red and black.

After much pressure on Pope Pius VII, Saint Napoleon, an early
Christian allegedly martyred by the emperor Diocletian, was
duly honoured every year on the 15 August birthday of his
illustrious namesake, Napoleon Bonaparte. To the Napoleonic
French Army, he became the patron saint of warriors. His blood
nephew, Bonaparte, even had his own image superimposed over
that of the saint on religious icons. Red and black are the
symbolic colours of death and blood, while green generally
symbolises life.

⧗ 1804 ⧗

Jamais par le descouvrement du jour
Ne parviendra au signe sceptrifere
Que tous ses sieges ne soient en sejour,
Portant du coq don du TAG amifere.

Never by sunrise
Will he reach the sign of the sceptre
Even if all sieges end
And he brings more armies to the Cock.

This is a royalist's reference to Napoleon's assumption of the title Emperor, in 1804. Nostradamus implies that Napoleon will never have the same right to rule as those with Royal blood, not even if he were to end all sieges and add to France's armies.

1805

De mer copies en trois parts divisees,
A la seconde les vivres failliront,
Desesperez cherchant champs Helisees,
Premier en breche entrez victoire auront.

The naval forces will be divided into three parts
The second force will lack supplies
In despair, they will seek Elysian fields
The first ones through the breach will snatch the victory.

Admiral Lord Horatio Nelson (1758–1805) fought and won the battle of Trafalgar on 21 October 1805, losing his life in the process. 'Three parts' refers to the three combatants, France, Spain and England. The Spanish vessels were known to have 'lacked supplies'. Nelson drove a 'breach' through both navies, 'snatching victory' (*Victory* was also the name of Nelson's flagship) by a margin of twenty French and Spanish ships sunk, to the loss of no English vessel.

🏺 1805 🏺

Entre deux mers dressera promontoire,
Qui puis mourra par le mors du cheval,
Le sien Neptune pliera voile noire,
Par Calpre et classe auprès de Rocheval

A promontory will lie between two seas
Someone will die by a horse's bit
Neptune's own will unfold a black sail
Via Gibraltar and a fleet close to Cape Roche.

The promontory must be Cape Trafalgar, which gave its name to the sea battle of 21 October 1805, fought between Gibraltar (Calpre) and Cape Roche. Nelson, the victor – Neptune's own – was killed, and was borne back to England in a ship rigged with a black sail. Admiral Villeneuve, commander of the vanquished French fleet, was captured. When released, he was ordered to Paris, but rather than face Napoleon, he hanged himself in a livery stable, possibly with his horse's bridle.

⌛ 1807 ⌛

Par cité franche de la grand mer Seline,
Qui porte encores à l'estomac la pierre
Angloise classe viendra soubs la bruine
Un rameau prendre, du grand ouverte guerre.

From the fair city of the great crescent sea
Which still carries the stone in its stomach
An English fleet will come through the fog
To seize one branch; war is declared by the great one.

Genoa is normally taken to be the 'city of the crescent sea', but the name could also be applied to Constantinople, known, since 1930, as Istanbul. In which case the 'English fleet' may refer to Admiral Sir John Thomas Duckworth's squadron, which appeared before Constantinople in 1807 and attempted to force the Dardanelles. The Turks succeeded in driving him out, with the loss of two of his ships.

⌛ 1807 ⌛

Les deux malins de Scorpion conjoinct,
Le grand seigneur meutri dedans sa salle
Peste à l'Eglise par le nouveau roy joinct
L'Europe basse et Septentrionale.

The two evil ones will join in Scorpio
The great Lord will be murdered in his hall
The new king will plague both the church
And Europe, north and south.

Mars and Saturn, the two evil ones, conjoined in Scorpio in 1807, when 'Seignior' Selim III of Turkey was deposed from his throne. He was murdered a year later. At the same time, in France, Napoleon was holding Pope Pius VII prisoner, following his defeat of Austria, Prussia and Russia.

⧗ 1808 ⧗

Bien contigue des grands monts Pyrenees
Un contre l'aigle grand copie addresser
Ouvertes veines, forces exterminées
Comme jusque à Pau le chef viendra chasser.

Near the great Pyrenees mountains
One man will raise a great army against the Eagle
Veins will be opened, soldiers exterminated
The chief will chase them as far as Pau.

Arthur Wellesley (1769–1852), later Duke of Wellington, was despatched to Portugal in 1808 to lead the war against the occupying French (as in Napoleon's Eagle) in the Iberian peninsular. After five years' fighting, British troops crossed into France in pursuit of the retreating occupying force.

1809

Terroir Romain qu'interpretoit Augure,
Par gent Gauloise par trop sera vexée.
Mais nation Celtique craindra l'heure,
Boreas classe trop loing l'avoir poussée.

Roman territory, comprising that of the Augur
Will be much troubled by the French
But the Celtic nation will not endure it this time
Their winter fleet will have pushed too far.

Napoleon Bonaparte annexed the Papal States (the Pope is seen as the successor to the Augur of ancient Rome). With his armies and fleets extended all over Europe and the Russian campaign looming, the Emperor will live to regret coming this far.

⧗ 1809 ⧗

Bien pres du Timbre presse la Lybitine
Un peu devant grand inondation
Le chef du nef prins, mis à la sentine
Chasteau, palais en conflagration.

The Death Goddess threatens very near to the Tiber
A short while before the great flood
The captain of the ship is put in the scuppers
Both the palace and castle are burnt down.

The river of Rome goes into flood and a palace and castle –
surely the Vatican – are burnt. The captain of the ship must be
the Pope, in this case Pope Pius VII, arrested by Napoleon. The
destruction of the Vatican is figurative – unless this quatrain
refers to some disaster yet to be visited upon the Holy See.

1809

Au sacrez temples seront faicts escandales,
Comptez seront par honneurs et louanges.
D'un que on grave d'argent, d'or les medalles,
La fin sera en torments bien estranges

There will be scandals in the churches
Some will be thought honest and praiseworthy
One, whose image is engraved on coins and medals
Will die, strangely tormented.

Napoleon and his persecution of the Italian clergy in 1809. Napoleon's image certainly appeared on the coins of the French realm, and he did die, on the isle of St Helena, tormented by stomach cancer.

Le divin mal surprendra le grand Prince,
Un peu devant aura femme espousée,
Son Appuy et credit à un coup viendra mince,
Conseil mourra la teste rasée.

God's vengeance will fall on the great Prince
Just before he will have taken a wife
Acclaim for him at this action will grow thin
Support will dry up for the shaven-headed one.

Nostradamus refers almost vindictively to Napoleon I in the last line, alluding to the undoubted fact that the great man went prematurely bald. The theme of the quatrain is clearly Napoleon's December 1809 divorce from the Empress Josephine, and the disapproval with which it was met. Napoleon immediately afterwards married the Arch-duchess Marie Louise of Austria.

1809

En naviguant captif prins grand Pontif,
Grand après faillier les clercs tumultuez:
Second esleu absent son bien debiffe,
Son favory bastard à mort tué.

While navigating, the great Pontif will be taken prisoner
In the aftermath the clergy will be in tumult
This second absent elected one will lose all
The false one he favoured will kill him.

Pope Pius VII traduced by Napoleon Bonaparte. The Pope
attended Napoleon's imperial coronation in 1804, thus favouring this false monarch. He was humiliated at the ceremony, and
opposed Napoleon thereafter. He was arrested by the French in
1809, a fate shared by his predecessor Pius VI, which made him
the second elected pope to be absent from Rome. Napoleon did
not have him killed; he was released in 1814 and returned to
Rome, where he died in 1823, aged 81.

⏳ 1812 ⏳

Amas s'approche venant d'Esclavonie,
L'Olestant vieux cité ruinera
Fort desolee verra sa Romanie.
Puis la grand flamme estaindre ne sçaura.

A mass of men will approach from Slavonia
The Destroyer will ruin an old city
He will see his dreams of empire shattered
He will not know how to extinguish the flames.

Napoleon Bonaparte arrived in Moscow on the night of 14 September 1812. While his soldiers camped in the deserted streets, citizens of the ancient wooden city raced around, setting fire to its buildings. The fires raged for five days, during which four fifths of the city was destroyed. Napoleon began his retreat from Moscow on 19 October, but the retreat turned into a rout after Marshal Kutuzov led the Russian army to victory at Smolensk, in November, against Marshals Ney and Davout.

1813

Quand le plus grand emportera le pris
De Nuremberg, d'Auspourg et ceux de Basle
Par Agrippine chef Frankfort repris
Traverseront par Flamant jusqu'au Gale.

When the great man carries off the prize
Of Nuremberg, Augsburg, and Basle
Frankfurt will be retaken by the leader of Cologne
They will cross Flanders into France.

King Frederick William III of Prussia called his people to arms against the French on 3 February 1813, beginning the process by which Germany contributed to the defeat of Napoleon, and subsequently became the dominant continental power in Europe.

En la campaigne sera si longue pluie
Et en la Pouille si grand siccité
Coq verra l'Aigle, l'aesle mal accompli
Par Lyon mise sera en extremité.

Heavy rains will dog the campaign
In Puglia there will be a drought
The Cock will see the Eagle, its wing unfinished
The Lion will drive it to the brink.

Napoleonic wars. Nostradamus often construes Napoleon as an eagle, and the cock would be expected to symbolise France. The lion is usually associated with Britain. The last campaigns of 1813 in the run-up to the crushing defeat of the French at Leipzig were conducted in an exceedingly wet autumn. As for drought in Puglia, this might symbolise Napoleon's loss of power in Italy as his king of Naples, Joachim Murat, went over to the Austrians in hope of saving his throne.

⧖ 1813 ⧖

Deux grans freres seront chassez d'Espaigne
L'aisné vaincu sous les monts Pyrenees
Rougir mer, rosne, sang lemam d'Alemaigne
Narbon, Blyterre, d'Agath contaminees.

Two great brothers will be driven from Spain
The elder will be beaten under the Pyrenees
The sea and the Rhone will redden with Genevan
    blood from Germany
Narbonne and Beziers will be contaminated by Agde.

Europe-wide conflict. The brothers driven from Spain could be Napoleon Bonaparte and his brother Joseph, whom the Emperor appointed to the country's throne during the French occupation until his defeat at Vittoria in 1813 – Joseph was, indeed, the elder brother.

Tous ceux de Iler seront dans la Moselle,
Mettant à mort tous ceux de Loyre et Seine,
Le cours marin viendra d'haute velle,
Quand l'Espagnol ouvrira toute veine.

Men of the Iller will be in the Mosel
Putting to death those of the Loire and Seine
The marine power will come near the high valley
When the Spanish will open every vein.

Napoleon is losing the war in 1813, caught in the pincer movement of attacks from Austria, Prussia and Spain. Nostradamus makes poetic use of river names to delineate the northern front: the Iller is a tributary of the Danube, so it is Germans who are killing those of the Loire and Seine – the French. The marine power, England, has conquered Spain and advances to the Pyrenees. Vengeful Spaniards in the allied force will kill everyone they find as they cross into France on 8 October.

L'aigle pousée entour de pavillions,
Par autres oiseaux d'entour sera chassée
Quand bruit des cymbees, tubes et sonaillons,
Rendront le sens de la dame insensée.

The eagle will be driven back to the tents
And chased by other, nearby birds
At the sound of the cymbals, the trumpets and the
    bells
Sense will be restored to the angry woman.

Napoleon, the Eagle, was driven back from Moscow during the winter of 1813–14, chased by the Imperial eagles of Russia, Austria and Prussia. The angry woman may refer either to France, in the shape of Marianne, the republican symbol, or to Josephine, Napoleon's discarded wife. He had their marriage annulled on the grounds of her supposed infertility.

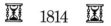 1814

Entre Bayonne et à Saint Jean de Lux
Sera posé de Mars la promottoire
Aux Hanix d'Aquilon Nanar hostera lux,
Puis suffocqué au lict sans adjutoire.

Between Bayonne and St Jean de Luz
Mars's promontory will be placed
Nanar will take the light from the unconquerable Northerners
He will be suffocated in bed, with no one to help him.

This accurately deals with the closing days of Napoleon's Empire in November 1814, when the Duke of Wellington crossed the Pyrenees with his Anglo-Spanish army and camped at St Jean de Luz. He later moved to besiege Marshal Soult's forces at Bayonne. 'Nanar', at a stretch, could be seen as an abbreviation for Napoleon Bonaparte. The Emperor died on the island of St Helena, on 5 May 1821, from stomach cancer. Could Nostradamus be implying that he was helped on his way?

⧗ 1814 ⧗

Au peuple ingrat faictes les remonstrances,
Par lors l'armee se saisira d'Antibe,
Dans l'arc Monech feront les doleances
Et à Frejus l'un l'autre prendra ribe.

Protests are made to the ungrateful people
Despite this, the army will seize Antibes
They will mourn in the Monegasque arch
And at Fréjus, one will seize the other's shore.

Antibes was the only town in France that remained loyal to
Napoleon after Louis XVIII issued a proclamation urging
fidelity to the crown. The ex-Emperor had used Antibes as his
embarkation point on his journey to exile in Elba.

1814

Les cinq estranges entrez dedans le temple,
Leur sang viendra la terre prophaner,
Aux Tholosains sera bien dur example
D'un qui viendra ses loys exterminer.

The five outsiders will enter within the temple
Their blood will profane the ground
Toulouse's people will be a hard example
From one who comes to extinguish their rights.

The five outsiders are the allies – Britain, Austria, Prussia, Russia and Spain – who will invade France. Toulouse did indeed suffer. The Duke of Wellington defeated a French army (under the command of his old adversary Marshal Soult) north-east of the city in one of the bloodiest battles of the occupation. The hardness of the example was the worse for the fact that the battle was completely unnecessary. Napoleon had already abdicated, but his commanders at Toulouse did not receive the news in time to effect a surrender.

⧗ 1815 ⧗

Le captif prince aux Itales vaincu
Passera Gennes par mer jusqu'à Marseille,
Par grand effort des forens survaincu
Sauf coup de feu barril liqueur d'abeille.

The beaten, captive prince, at Elba
Will cross by sea from Genoa to Marseilles
He is overcome, after much effort, by foreigners
Safe from assassination, a barrel of bee's liquor.

One of several quatrains mentioning Napoleon's 'bee' emblem.
With commendable detail, it tells of Napoleon's final hundred
days, in 1815, his escape by sea, from Elba, the 'effort' entailed in
his march up through France, and his nemesis at Waterloo.

Nice sortie sur nom des lettres aspres
La grande cappe sera present son sien
Proche de Vultry aux murs de vertes capres
Apres plombin le vent à bon essien.

Leaving Nice in the name of the bitterly-worded letters
The great caped one will stay with his own people
Near Voltri, at the walls of the green corsairs
The wind will get up beyond Piombino.

Capres in line 3 has nearly always been mistranslated as capers but it actually means corsair in old French, or one who travels in a corsair. It can now be seen to apply to Napoleon, who set sail in a corsair from near Piombino during his flight from exile in Elba, in February 1815. He began his seventeen day march to Paris from behind Nice, on what is now the Route Napoleon, entering the capital on 19 March.

⧖ 1815 ⧖

Le croisé frere par amour effrenee
Fera par Praytus Bellesophon mourir,
Classe à mil ans la femme forcenee,
Beu le breuvage, tous deux apres perir.

The crusading brother, loving fervently
Will cause Bellerophon, through Proteus, to die
The imprisoned woman, and the thousand year army
The potion will be drunk, both will later die.

The myth of Bellerophon and Proteus deals with the dangers of
vanity. The goddess Athena gave Bellerophon the horse Pegasus
with which to kill the Chimera. Later, wishing to boast of his
prowess, Bellerophon was lamed when Zeus sent a gadfly to
sting his mount. Napoleon was exiled to St Helena on board the
Bellerophon, in 1815. Slowly dying of stomach cancer, Napoleon
chose to think that he was being poisoned by the British. He too,
had been brought down by a surfeit of vanity.

⧖ 1815 ⧖

Par grans dangiers le captif eschapé,
Peu de temps grand a fortune changée
Dans le palais le peuple est attrapé,
Par bon augure la cité assiegée.

The prisoner escaped, braving great danger
Soon the great one sees his fortune changed
The people are trapped inside the palace
By good luck, the city is besieged.

Napoleon escaped from Elba on 1 March 1815. Faced with the bayonets of the Fifth Infantry regiment barring his route to Grenoble, Napoleon risked his life by confronting the soldiers. Despite their commander giving the order to fire, Napoleon succeeded in convincing the regiment to mutiny against their leader, Louis XVIII. Arriving in Paris, Napoleon was carried to the Royal Apartments on the shoulders of the crowd, which was so large that people were trapped inside the palace for hours.

⧗ 1815 ⧗

Par faim la proye fera loup prisonnier,
L'assaillant lors en extreme detresse,
Le nay ayant au devant le dernier,
Le grand n'eschappe au milieu de la presse.

Wild with hunger, the quarry will imprison the wolf
Causing its attacker great distress
With the young preceding the old
The great man cannot escape, hidden by the crowd.

'*Le nay*' in line three, may well apply to Marshall Ney (1769–1815), whose gallant but ultimately futile efforts on the battle-field of Waterloo may have gone some way towards costing Napoleon his expected victory. Napoleon, the 'great man', did not escape in the midst of his troops, but was swiftly made a prisoner by the English and sent on his way to final exile in St Helena.

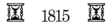 1815

Au mois troisième se levant le Soleil
Sanglier, Leopard, aux champs Mars pour combatre
Leopard lasse au Ciel estena son oeil,
Un Aigle autour du Soleil voit sesbatre.

At the sun's rise in the third month
The wild boar and leopard are in the battlefield
The leopard left alone, raises his eyes to heaven
An eagle is seen to fight against the sun.

Waterloo, 15 June 1815, a hundred days (three months) after Napoleon Bonaparte landed back on French soil. The leopard, Britain, has determined to make a stand here to face the French. Wellington anxiously awaits his ally the boar – Blücher, at the head of the Prussian forces. The imperial eagles of Napoleon's army came first, out of the sun, and battle was joined.

1815

L'ensevely sortira du tombeau,
Fera de chaines lier de fort du pont:
Empoysoné avec oeuf de barbeau,
Grand de lorraine par le Marquis du Pont.

The buried one leaves his grave
He will forge the links of a strong bridge
Poisoned with fish roe
Is the big man of Lorraine by the Marquis du Pont.

The significant line is said to be the first, predicting the restoration of the Bourbon monarchy after Napoleon's defeat at Waterloo. The buried one is Louis XVIII, who had been restored in the previous year, but looked politically dead when Napoleon escaped from Elba and returned to France.

⧗ 1815 ⧗

Du bourg Lareyne ne parviendront droit à Chartres
Et feront pres du pont Anthoni panse
Sept pour la paix cantelleux comme martres
Feront entrée d'armee à Paris clause.

They won't come straight to Chartres from
    Bourg-la-Reine
They will pause near Pont d'Antony
Seven, as crafty as martens, are for peace
Armed, they will enter tightly-sealed Paris.

The seven allied nations of England, Prussia, Portugal, Austria, Sweden, Spain and Russia entered Paris on 3 July 1815, following Napoleon's final defeat at the Battle of Waterloo on 18 June. As per its agreement, the main French Army had already pulled back through Bourg-la-Reine, on its way to Chartres. To further leaven the success of this quatrain, the army is even said to have camped beneath the Pont d'Antony.

1815

Heureux au regne de France, heureux de vie,
Ignorant sang, mort, fureur et rapine,
Par nom flatteur sera mis en envie:
Roy desrobé, trop de foye en cuisine.

Happy on the throne of France, happy in life
Ignorant of blood, death, fury and plunder
Flattered by a name the speaks of desire
A king without majesty, too interested in food.

King Louis XVIII of France. Brother of the executed Louis XVI, he escaped the Revolution and found comfortable sanctuary in England, far from the tribulations of war. Restored after Napoleon's defeat, he was happy indeed, and had the popular nickname Le Désiré, signifying the strength of feeling with which so many in France had awaited the restoration. A notorious glutton, Louis was a good deal more interested in matters of the table than he was in matters of state.

Chef de Fosan aura gorge coupee,
Par le ducteur du limier et laurier
La faict patre par ceux de mont Tarpee,
Saturne en Leo 13 de Fevrier.

A leader from Fossano will have his throat slit
By one who trains hounds
The deed is done by a criminal
When Saturn is in Leo, on the 13 February.

Another remarkable dating, this time to the assassination of the Duke de Berry, on 13 February 1820. Berry's maternal grandfather was the King of Fossano, in Sardinia. Louvel, Berry's assassin, was a Republican, and worked in the Royal stables, thus the reference to the Tarpean Rock, from which Republican Rome was wont to throw her criminals. Louvel stabbed the Duke on his exit from the Opera.

🏺 1820 🏺

L'arbre qu'estoit par long temps mort seché,
Dans une nuict viendra à reverdir
Cron Roy malade, Prince pied estaché,
Criant d'ennemis fera voile bondir.

A tree, which had for a long time been thought dead
  of drought
Will flourish again, in the course of one night
The old sick king and the prince with one leg
Will set sail, fearing enemies.

The Duchess of Berry gave birth to a son on 29 September 1820, seven months after her husband was assassinated, thus ensuring the continuation of the Bourbon line. The boy later injured his leg falling from a horse, causing him a permanent limp. He and his grandfather, Charles X, were forced into exile in 1830, and he never succeeded to the throne of France.

⌛ 1821 ⌛

Cent fois mourra le tyran inhumain;
Mis à son lieu scavant et debonnaire,
Tout le Senat sera dessous sa main,
Fasché sera par malin temeraire.

A hundred deaths the inhuman tyrant will die
Replaced by a scholarly and debonair man
The government will be in his thrall
He will be troubled by wicked temerity.

Napoleon Bonaparte died the last of his hundred deaths after a miserable six years' confinement on St Helena in 1821. Louis XVIII, who was scholarly and debonair by any standards, had a good start to his reign, but later years were marred by the assassination of his nephew, an heir to the throne.

1824

Quand dans la regne parviendra la boiteux,
Competiteur aura proche bastard
Lui et le regne viendront si fort roigneux,
Qu'ains qu'il guerisse son faict sera bien tard.

When the lame man achieves the kingdom
His close competitor will be a bastard
Both he and the kingdom will become mean
So that, when he recovers, his actions will come too late.

Franklin D. Roosevelt has been nominated for the lame man, as
has the Duke of Bordeaux, heir of Charles X of France. The
trouble is, neither of them recovered. The most famous poet in
Europe, Lord Byron (1788–1824), was also lame, and certainly
achieved the kingdom, if only by notoriety. He sailed to Greece
at the end of his life with the intention of helping the Greeks
shake off Turkish rule, and died at Missolonghi on 19 April 1824.

Le camp du temple de la vierge vestale
Non esloigné d'Ethne et monte Pyrenées
Le grand conduict est caché dans la male
North getez fleuves et vignes mastinées.

The field of the Vestal Virgin's Temple
Not far from Ethne and the Pyrenees
The great one led and hidden in a tree trunk
In the North the rivers overflow and vines are bruised.

A reference to Tibur, now Tivoli, north-east of Rome, the site of the spectacular Villa d'Este, started in 1549 (no doubt to Nostradamus's knowledge) by the architect Pirro Ligorio for Cardinal Ipoolito d'Este. Tivoli narrowly escaped complete destruction in November 1826 when the river Arnio flooded disastrously, washing away large expanses of vineyards and olive groves. The references to Vestal Virgins and the Pyrenees are thinly veiled disguises for the name Este and the Sabine mountains, through whih the river Arnio flows.

1830

De nuict dans lict le supresme estrangle,
Par trop avoir sejourné, blond esleu
Par trois l'empire subrogé exanche,
A mort mettra carte, et pacquet ne leu.

The last one is strangled in his bed, at night
For having spent too much time with the blonde
    pretender
The empire is enslaved by three substitutes
His death occurs with the Will still unread.

The last in the line of Bourbon-Condés was found hanging in
his bedroom. His assassins had strangled him in his bed, then
hung him with a rope to conceal the marks of their deed. The
substitutes in question are Louis Philippe, Napoleon III and the
Third Republic of Thiers and MacMahon. Condé had written a
will, but it was destroyed by his assassins and replaced with a
new one, favouring the Duke of Aumale, son of Louis Philippe.

1830

Celuy qu'en Sparte Claude ne peut regner,
Il fera tant par voye seductive,
Que de court, long le fera araigner,
Que contre Roy fera sa perspective.

He who cannot reign as Claude in Sparta
Will do much by way of seduction
In a short time, after long conspiring
The King will prevail over views against him.

Possibly a view of the events of July 1830 in Paris. The reigning king, Charles X, was forced to abdicate in the *Révolution de Juillet* because he could not reconcile his notions of divine right with those of the democratic ambitions of his nation. His place was taken by the 'Citizen King' Louis-Philippe. The reference to Sparta is a witty allegory of a state once ruled by two kings at once.

Cris, pleurs, larmes viendront avec coteaux
Semblant fouir donront dernier assault.
Lentour parques planter profons plateaux,
Vifs repoulsez et meurdris de prinsault.

Cries, weeping, tears, come with the knives
Pretending to flee, they will make one last assault
They will set up high platforms around the parks
The living are repulsed, and straightway murdered.

This harks back to the Fall of Troy, and the Greeks use of the Trojan Horse. 'Trojan' was often used by Nostradamus as a euphemism for the French Royal house. Is he foretelling the slow downfall of the French monarchy? If so, the image is accurate. The monarchy raised itself a number of times, before finally bowing its head before the unstoppable Republican onslaught in 1830.

Prince libinique puissant en Occident
François d'Arabe viendra tant enflammer
Scavans aux lettres sera condescendant
La langue Arabe en François translater.

This Libyan Prince will be powerful in the West
The French will become enamoured of Arabia
A learned man, he will condescend
To translate the Arab tongue into French.

The French colonisation of north Africa came about by accident. On 14 June 1830, after a series of military skirmishes and diplomatic tiffs between Paris and Algiers, French troops were landed in Algeria with a view to persuading the ruler to desist from supporting corsairs in their attacks on French shipping in the Mediterranean. In the ensuing war, the French found themselves in possession of a valuable overseas territory. The translator may be Si-Hamza of the Walid-sidi-Sheikh family, who remained a loyal ally of France until his death in 1861.

Plus ne sera le grand en faux sommeil,
L'inquietude viendra prendre repoz
Dresser phalange d'or, azur, et vermeil,
Subjuger Affrique la ronger jusques oz.

No longer will the great man pretend to sleep
Unease will take the place of rest
A phalanx of gold, blue and vermillion will be raised
To subdue Africa and gnaw it to the very bone.

In 1830 Louis Philippe usurped the French crown, becoming the first Bourbon to accept the 'tricolour' flag. In an effort to popularise himself with the French people he invaded and conquered Algeria, storing up much trouble for the century to come.

1830

Sept ans sera Philipp. fortune prospere:
Rabaissera des Arabes l'effort;
Puis son midi perplex, rebors affaire,
Jeune Oignon abismera son fort.

For seven years Philipp's fortunes will prosper
He will humble Arab ambitions
His middle years will face a perplexing affair
Young Onion will reduce his strength.

King Louis-Philippe had an excellent start to his reign as the
Citizen King of France from 1830–38 but there were then
political troubles in the Middle East. The curious reference to
the Young Onion is extremely intriguing. Ogmiom was the
classical hero depicted on the five-centime coins minted by the
young Republic of 1848, which brought Louis-Philippe's reign
to an end.

⌛ 1836 ⌛

De ce grand nombre que l'on envoyera
Pour secourir dans le fort assiegez
Peste et famine tous les devorera
Hors mis septante qui seront profligez.

Of the great number sent
To relieve the captured fort
Disease and hunger will devour them all
Save seventy, who will die in other ways.

In the war for possession of Texas in 1836, the capture by 5,000 troops under the command of Mexican tyrant Santa Anna of a fort at the Alamo, now occupies a special place in American history. The garrison at the Alamo on 6 March 1836 consisted of 183 men, including Colonel William Bowie and the frontiersman Davy Crockett. It is said that Santa Anna lost a thousand men in taking the fort. All the garrison were slaughtered.

⌛ 1837–1901 ⌛

Le regne humain d'Anglique geniture,
Fera son regne paix union tenir,
Captive guerre demi de sa closture,
Long temps la paix leur fera maintenir.

The human throng, governed from England
Its reign will hold in peace and union
Half its extent will have been captured by war
For a long time, peace will be maintained for them.

Victorian England (1837–1901) can be accounted the heyday of the British Empire, during which peace 'reigned' or 'was maintained' for many long years. At its height Britain controlled nearly a quarter of the world's land area and population. Despite occasional lapses, the Empire was largely benevolent, and depended on trading and diplomacy rather than on military threats for its survival.

⧗ 1842 ⧗

L'aisné Royal sur coursier voltigeant,
Picquer viendra si rudement courir
Gueulle, lipee, pied dans l'estrein pleignant
Trainé, tiré, horriblement mourir.

The Royal eldest, on a leaping horse
Will spur it so badly that it bolts
Mouth, lips, foot will be injured in the stirrup
Dragged, pulled horribly to his death.

A grim prognosis for a royal heir – and indeed the fate on 13 July 1842 of Ferdinand Philippe, eldest son of King Louis-Philippe of France, who was killed when he fell from his carriage, catching his foot in the door, as the horses bolted.

Du Trumvir seront trouvez les os,
Cherchant profond tresor aenigmatique,
Ceux d'alentour ne seront en repos
Ce concaver marbre et plomb metallique.

The bones of the Triumvir will be found
In the deep search for an enigmatic treasure
Those in attendance will have no rest
In hollowing out marble and metal of lead.

Napoleon Bonaparte's remains are brought from St Helena to
the Invalides in Paris. He was a 'triumvir' in the sense that he
was one of three members of the Directory left in power by the
coup d'état of 1801.

Du vrai rameau de fleur de lys issue
Mis et logé heretier de Hetrurie
Son sang antique de long main tissu
Fera Florence florir en l'armoirie.

Born of the true branch of the fleur de lys
Put in place as the heir of Etruria
His noble and ancient blood
Will cause Florence's coat of arms to flourish.

Presumptive heir to King Charles X (1757–1836), but with his legitimacy questioned, the Count of Chambord was exiled to Venice with his mother, the Duchess of Berry. In 1846 he married the daughter of Duke Francis IV of Florence, thereby joining the *'fleur de lis'* of the French coat of arms to the *'fleur de lis'* of Florence, both of which flourished, effectively completing Nostradamus's pun.

⧗ 1846 ⧗

Au deserteur de la grand fortresse,
Apres qu'aura son lieu abandonné
Son adversaire fera si gran prouesse,
L'Empereur tost mort sera condamné.

The one who left the great fortress
Some time after he abandons his post
Will see his adversary display such great skill
That the emperor, soon to die, will be condemned.

On 25 May 1846, Louis Napoleon (1808–73), later Napoleon III, escaped to England from the fortress of Ham. Louis Philippe (1773–1850) abandoned his kingship of France during the 1848 revolution, after which Louis Napoleon was voted Prince President. He was later held responsible for the Franco-Prussian war and its disastrous effects on France, in which his adversaries undoubtedly displayed great skill.

1847

Le chef du camp au milieu de la presse
D'un coup de fleche sera blessé aux cuisses
Lors que Geneve eu larmes et detresse
Sera trahi par Lozan et Souisses.

The leader of the army, standing in a crowd
Will be injured in the thigh by an arrow
At the same time distressed and troubled Geneva
Will be betrayed by Lausanne and the Swiss.

Switzerland, troubled by strife between Calvinist protestants and militant Catholics almost continuously since the Reformation, was plunged into a civil war in November 1847 as a league of Catholic cantons rebelled against the rule of the federal government. But the cantons were violently put down and surrendered within weeks. The wounding of their leader was not with the arrow of Nostradamus's vision, but with a Swiss-made firearm.

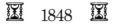 1848

Par le rameau du vaillant personnage
De France infime, par le pere infelice
Honneurs, richesses, travail en son vieil aage
Pour avoir creu le conseil d'homme nice.

The offspring of the brave person
Becomes infamous in France, his father unhappy
Honours, riches, much work in old age
All because he believed an inexperienced man.

Son of the Duke of Orléans, Louis Philippe was elected King of France in 1830, but failed in his role of 'citizen monarch' by accepting bad advice that he should retain his hold on the crown through censorship and the abolition of trial by jury. He was unseated, at the age of seventy-five, in the revolution of 1848.

Après le siege tenu dix-sept ans,
Cinq changeront en tel revolu terme:
Puis sera l'un esleu de mesme temps,
Qui des Romains ne sera trop conforme.

After keeping his seat for 17 years
Five will change in a similar period
Then one will be elected at the same time
Who will not conform closely to the Romans.

King Louis-Philippe's reign in France ended in its seventeenth year with the Revolution of 1848, disinheriting five princes. The elected one is Louis Napoleon, nephew of Napoleon Bonaparte, who became President of the Republic that year and Emperor in 1852. He conducted military campaigns in Italy.

⧗ 1848 ⧗

Par le decide de deux choses bastards,
Nepveu du sang occupera le regne,
Dedans lectoure seront les coups de dards.
Nepveu par pleira l'enseigne.

By the demise of two illegitimate things
The nephew of the blood will have the realm
History will speak of him in forked tongues
The nephew will bend to the signs.

Following two illegitimate governments in France (those of King Louis-Philippe and the Second Republic) the nephew takes over – Louis Napoleon, son of Napoleon Bonaparte's brother Louis. Later Emperor, his reign was ended by his unwise declaration of war against Prussia in July 1870.

⌛ 1856 ⌛

Ambassadeur de la Toscane langue
Avril et May Alpes et mer passer,
Celuy de veau exposera harangue,
Vie Gauloise ne venant effacer.

The Tuscan-speaking Ambassador
Crosses the Alps and sea in April and May
He of the calf will expose in a harangue
That France is incompatible.

A reference to attempts made by Italy to obtain independence of French and Austrian influence and to find its own unity. The Ambassador was Camillo Benso, Count of Cavour, representing Victor Emmanuel, the future Italian King, whose centre of power was Turin – the city of the bull.

Peuple assemblé, voir nouveau epectacle
Princes et Rois par plusieurs assistans
Pilliers faillir, murs, mais comme miracle
Le Roi sauvé et trente des instants.

People are assembled to see the spectacle
Princes and Kings with several aides
Walls and pillars fall, but miraculously
The King is saved, and thirty bystanders.

Italian republican Felice Orsini's attempt on the life of
Napoleon III on 14 January 1858. Orsini's bomb killed eight
bystanders and wounded more than a hundred in the crowd
gathered outside the Paris Opera. The building was badly
damaged, but the Emperor and his consort Empress Eugenie,
along with others, escaped injury.

🏺 1859 🏺

Dela les Alpes grande armée passera,
Un peu devant naistra monstre vapin;
Prodigieux et subit tournera
Le grand Toscan à son lieu plus propin.

A great army will pass beyond the Alps
Shortly before, a consuming monster will arise
Suddenly and prodigiously it will turn out
That the great Tuscan will return home.

Napoleon III of France invaded Italy in 1859, driving the Grand
Duke of Tuscany, Leopold II, a Habsburg, back to Austria where
he came from. The consuming monster is the *Risorgimento*.

⌛ 1860 ⌛

La gent esclave par un heur martial
Viendra en haut degré tant esleuee
Changeront prince, naistre un provincial
Passer la mer copie aux monts levee.

The slave people, through good fortune in war
Will become so highly elevated
That they will change their prince, born in the provinces
An army raised in the mountains will cross the sea.

Abraham Lincoln was elected President of the United States in 1860 on an anti-slavery ticket. But the Confederacy of seven southern states would not submit to national policy on the matter of abolition and withdrew from the Union in the following year, pitching America into a bitter civil war. Lincoln was assassinated but the Union triumphed, and on 6 April 1866 all people in the United States were guaranteed liberty under the Civil Rights Act. Lincoln confessed to a recurring dream that he was moving across water to a dark and distant shore.

⧗ 1860 ⧗

Du grand Prophete les lettres seront prinses.
Entre les mains du tyran deviendront,
Frauder son Roy seront ses entreprinses,
Mais ses rapines bien tost le troubleront.

The great Prophet's writings will be seized
They will come into the hands of the tyrant
His purposes will be to cheat his King
But soon his plunderings will trouble him.

In 1860, a leading Nostradamus interpreter, the Abbé Torné, published a volume entitled *L'Histoire prédité et jugée* in which he clearly predicted that Napoleon III of France would be deposed. The Emperor ordered the book confiscated on the grounds it was seditious.

⧗ 1860 ⧗

Mars esleue en son plus haut befroi,
Fera retraire les Allobrox de France
La gent Lombarde fera si grand effroi,
A ceux de l'aigle comprins souz la Balance.

A mighty warrior, raised high
Will restore the Savoyards to France
The Lombardians will cause much terror
To the Eagle's followers, including the Librans.

Savoy belonged to France at the time Nostradamus was writing,
so here he is predicting not only its loss, which occurred in 1559,
but also its eventual restoration, which took place 301 years
later, on 22 March 1860, when King Victor-Emmanuel II
presented Savoy to Napoleon III in gratitude for French help
against the Austrians (the Librans).

Perdu, trouvé caché de si long siècle
Sera Pasteur demi-Dieu honoré,
Ainsi que la Lune achève son grand siècle,
Par autre vents fera dishonoré.

Lost but found hidden for long centuries
Pasteur will be honoured as a demi-god
Just as the moon reaches her high point
Other opinions will revile him.

Nostradamus looks three centuries ahead to the work of a figure he may well have seen as his own natural successor, Louis Pasteur (1822–95). The great French chemist was the father of bacteriology. From 1865 onwards, he revealed how diseases such as plague were spread by micro-organisms. He was indeed elevated to the highest status by the scientific community – although he had his detractors elsewhere.

1867

Gens d'alentour de Tarn Loth, et Garonne
Gardez les monts Apennines passer
Vostre tombeau pres de Rome et d'Anconne
Le noir poil crespe fera trophee dresser.

You people from the Tarn, the Lot and the Garonne
Don't cross the Appenine mountains
Your tomb will be near Rome and Ancona
The man with the dark curly hair will triumph.

France is warned not to invade Italy, but it was a French force that prevented Giuseppe Garibaldi (1807–82) seizing Rome in 1867. Garibaldi's *Risorgimento,* the rise of united Italy, triumphed in the end, and the revolutionary made his peace with France, being elected a deputy to the Bordeaux Assembly in later life.

⌛ 1870 ⌛

De feu celeste au Royal edifice
Quant la lumiere de Mars defaillira
Sept mois grand guerre, mort gent de malefice
Rouen, Eureux au Roi ne faillira.

Fire will fall from the sky on to the Royal building
Just as the war is weakening
Seven months the great war lasted, many evil killings
Rouen and Evreux will not fail the king.

The Franco-Prussian War of 1870–71, in which the Palace of the Tuileries in Paris was submitted to artillery fire. The war, declared by France on Prussia on 16 July 1870, was ended seven months later by a provisional treaty signed on 26 February 1871 at Versailles. While much of France capitulated to the Prussian invasion immediately, Normandy towns such as Rouen supported the king, Napoleon III. An astonishingly astute prophecy in every respect.

Des lieux plus bas du pays de Lorraine
Seront les basses Allemaignes unis,
Par ceux du siege Picards, Normans, du Maine,
Et aux cantons se seront reunis.

Regions south of Lorraine
Will be united to southern Germany
By the besieged of Picardy, Normandy and Maine
And they will be reunited to the cantons.

The Franco-Prussian war. The Prussians' first thrusts were into precisely the regions mentioned.

⧗ 1870 ⧗

La garde estrange trahira forteresse
Espoir et umbre de plus hault mariage
Garde deçeue, fort prince dans la presse,
Loire, Son, Rosne. Gar à mort oultrage.

The foreign guard will betray the fortress
There will be hope, the shadow of an all-powerful conjunction
With the guards deceived, the fort will be stormed, then taken
The Loire, the Saone, the Rhone and the Garonne, all
    mortally outraged.

The capitulation of Metz took place in 1870. General Bazaine retreated there, rather than taking advantage of his defeat of the Prussians at St Privat and Gravelotte. His decision allowed the Prussian troops access to the interior of France. During his court-martial, in 1872, accusations were made that he had received bribes from the Prussians.

⧗ 1870–1 ⧗

Sous un la paix par tout sera clamee
Mais non long temps pillé et rebellion
Par refus ville, terre, et mer entamee,
Mors et captifs le tiers d'un million.

Thanks to one man, peace will be declared
Though soon afterwards there will be riot and looting
Because of pride, both city, land and sea will be
    broached
And a third of a million killed, or taken captive.

This refers to Napoleon III of France's statement *'L'Empire c'est la paix,'* indicating that he considered his Second Empire the empire of peace. However, following Kaiser Wilhelm I of Prussia's refusal to accede to France's humiliating demands relating to Hohenzollern rights to the Spanish throne, the Prussians declared war on an unprepared France. Between 300,000 and 350,000 people were killed in the ensuing fighting.

⧗ 1879 ⧗

L'enfant Royal contemnera la mère
Oeil, pieds blessez, rude, inobeisant.
Nouvelle à dame estrange et bien amere,
Seront tuez des siens plus que cinq cens.

The Royal child, disdains his mother
Defiant, footloose, hard, disobedient
News to the foreign lady is very bitter
He and 500 of his men will be killed.

The death of the Prince Imperial, son of Napoleon III of France, at the hands of Zulus in South Africa, in 1879. Exiled to Chislehurst in Kent, the Emperor had died in 1873 and the Empress was very reluctant to let her son join the English expedition against the Zulus (the prince had been educated at Woolwich), but he defied her and was killed in battle – with 530 of his comrades. With him died all hopes of a restoration of the Napoleonic dynasty to the throne of France.

Le grand naistra de Veronne et Vicence,
Qui portera un surnam bien indigne,
Qui a Venise voudra faire vengeance,
Luy mesme prins homme de guet et fine.

The great one will be born of Verona and Vicenza
Who will bear a very undignified surname
Who at Venice will wish to gain vengeance
But will himself be taken by a sharp and wary man.

Benito Mussolini was born in the Romagna in 1883, the son of a blacksmith, whose name means maker of muslin. When he later became dictator of Italy, Mussolini met Adolf Hitler in Venice to discuss an alliance that would help Italy avenge past defeats by European enemies. But Hitler was not a man with whom a wise statesman made agreements for any purpose.

Predictions of Nostradamus for the
18th CENTURY

Croix, paix, soubz un accompli divin verbe
L'Espaigne et Gaule seront unis ensemble
Grand clade proche, et combat tresacerbe
Coeur si hardi ne sera qui ne tremble.

Peace and the cross achieved through divine word
Spain and France are unified
A great disaster looms, the fighting will be ferocious
Even brave hearts will tremble.

The union of France and Spain, a principal ambition of Louis XIV of France, would have taken place in 1700 on the death of Spain's King Charles II, but for the intervention of European states concerned at the consequences for the balance of power. The War of Spanish Succession ensued.

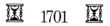 **1701**

Par mort la France prendra voyage à faire,
Classe par mer, marcher monts Pyrenées,
Espaigne en trouble, marcher gent militaire,
Des plus grands Dames en France emmenées.

Death will lead France to make a voyage
Ships will sail, the Pyrenees will be crossed
Spain will experience a military invasion
The greatest ladies will be brought into France.

The War of the Spanish Succession arose from King Louis XIV of France's belief that his marriage to the daughter of a Spanish king entitled him to that country's throne – as confirmed in the will of Spain's Charles II, who died in 1700. The rest of Europe was not convinced that the union of two nations as powerful as France and Spain would be entirely beneficial to the balance of power, and war broke out in the following year.

⧗ 1701–14 ⧗

L'Aemathion passer montz Pyrenees
En Mars Narbon ne fera resistance
Par mer et terre fera si grand menee
Cap. n'ayant terre seure pour demeurance.

The Aemathian will cross the Pyrenees in March
Narbonne will not resist
He will carry his intrigues by land and sea
The Capets will have nowhere left to hide.

Aemathion may refer either to Louis XIV (the Sun King) or to a
man with a Macedonian name (possibly his grandson, Philip
V). During the 1701–14 War of the Spanish Succession Philip
fought against the Grand Alliance of England, the Netherlands,
Denmark, Austria and Portugal, for his right to the Spanish
throne. The matter was finally settled, to nobody's satisfaction,
in the Treaty of Utrecht.

Le grand Prélat Celtique à Roy suspect,
De nuict par cours sortira hors de regne,
Par Duc fertile à son Grand Bretaine,
Bisance a Cypres et Tunes insuspect.

The great French Prelate suspected by the King
Will leave the kingdom in haste by night
Enabled by the conquering Duke to Great Britain
Undetected through Bisance, Cyprus and Tunis.

Since the 18th century, this has been believed to refer to the escape of the Cardinal de Bouillon from his master, King Louis XIV of France. The Cardinal was aided by the Duke of Marlborough, who spirited him to Britain via a (very) circuitous route.

⌛ 1712 ⌛

Par les Sueves et lieux circonvoisins,
Seront en guerre pour cause des nuees
Gamp marins locustes et cousins,
Du Leman fautes seront bien desnuees.

Through Switzerland and its surrounding area
A war will be fought, on account of the clouds
From the sea will come locusts and gnats
Geneva's faults will be open to scrutiny.

There have been very few wars fought over Swiss soil, but Swiss Protestants and Catholics did clash on a number of occasions, culminating in the Bernese triumph at Villmergen, on 25 July 1712, which established the dominance of the Protestant cantons. Clouds may therefore be taken as a euphemism for spiritual matters. It should be remembered that John Calvin (1509–1564), the 'gnat' sucking the blood of Catholicism, had lived in Geneva for two years, from 1536 to 1538.

La cité franche de liberté fait serve,
Des profligés et resveurs faict asile
Le Roy changé à eux non si proterve
De cent seront devenus plus de mille.

The free and democratic city will be enslaved
Becoming and asylum for the corrupt and feckless
A change of king makes things easier for them
From a hundred, they become a thousand.

There were many free cities in Europe during the sixteenth century, but Nostradamus is referring here to Orange, which was only ceded to the French in 1713. Before then it was a haven for French Protestants, whom Nostradamus would certainly have defined as corrupt and feckless.

Une nouvelle secte de Philosophes
Mesprisant mort, or, honneurs et richesses
Des monts Germains ne seront limitrophes
A les ensuivre auront appuy et presses.

A new sect of philosophers
Scorning death, gold, honours and riches
They will refuse to confine themselves to the German mountains
They will have the support of many people.

A marvellous prediction of the *Philosophes*, France's great men of letters – led by Denis Diderot (1713–84) and followed up by the likes of Jean-Jacques Rousseau and Voltaire – whose writings on political philosophy in the eighteenth century inspired the new age of materialism, religious scepticism and interest in popular democracy. France under the Bourbons was inimical to many of these men's ideas, and they regularly sought refuge and sponsorship abroad. Diderot was supported by Catherine the Great of Russia and Voltaire by Frederick the Great of Prussia.

Un dubieux ne viendra loing du regne
La plus grand part le voudra soustenir
Un Capitole ne voudra point qu'il regne
Sa grande charge ne pourra maintenir.

A doubtful man will approach the kingdom
The greater part will wish to support him
The Pope will not want him to reign
He will not be able to support his great burden.

The accession of George I, Elector of Hanover, to the newly (1707) United Kingdom of Great Britain and Ireland in 1714. King George I was the great grandson of King James I of England, but spoke not a word of English. His succession to Queen Anne was not universally popular, but as a Protestant he was preferred to the other claimants, the Roman Catholic Stuarts – whom the Pope would of course have wished to see on the throne. The king never learned English and hated England.

Ce grand monarque qu'au mort succedera,
Donnera vie illicite et lubrique,
Par nonchalance à tous concedera,
Qu'à la parfin faudra la loi Salique.

He who succeeds, following the death of the great
    monarch
Will lead an illicit and lubricious life
Not caring, he will make many concessions
Leading to the failure of Salic law.

Louis XV (1710–1774) was recognised, after his death, as the most
wayward and decadent of all French kings. Succeeding his great-
grandfather, Louis XIV, in 1715, at the age of five, he later undid
the great king's legacy and laid the foundations for what would
eventually become the French Revolution. The failure of Salic
Law refers to his arrogation of power to Madame de Pompadour
and Madame du Barry, who metaphorically became sovereigns
in his stead, something illegal under the law.

⧖ 1715 ⧖

Coeur, vigueur, gloire, le regne changera,
De tous points contre ayant son adversaire:
Lors France enfance par mort subjuguera,
Un grand Regent sera lors plus contraire.

Heart, vigour, glory, the rule will change
In all ways against having his adversary
Then a child will come to power by death
A powerful Regent will then be more contrary.

Nostradamus looks forward with misgivings to the appointment
of a Regent, Philippe, Duke of Orléans, to rule on behalf of
Louis XV – who succeeded to the French throne aged only five
on the death of his great-grandfather, the brave, vigorous and
glorious Louis XIV. Orléans was a cultured man, but led a
scandalous private life; he was suspected of complicity in the
deaths of both previous heirs to the throne, Louis XV's father
and grandfather.

D'un chef vieillard naistra sens hébeté,
Degenerant par scavoir et par armes,
Le chef de France par sa soeur redouté,
Champs divisez, concedez aux gens l'armes.

To an old chief will be born a dullard
Degenerating in knowledge and arms
The chief of France, feared by his sister
Divides in the battlefield, conceding to men of arms.

The old chief is Louis XIV, who reigned from 1638 until his death in 1715 aged seventy-seven. He outlived his direct heirs and was succeeded by his great-grandson, five-year-old Louis XV, whose own long reign of thirty-nine years was marked by good intentions and disastrous policies at home and abroad. France suffered humiliating military defeats through much of the reign, and the prestige of the monarchy reached a new nadir under his tenure.

1722

De bois la garde, vent clos rond pont sera,
Haut le reçu frappera le Dauphin,
Le vieux teccon bois uni passera,
Passant plus outre du Duc le droit confin.

Dubois the guard, closed shutters in the apse
Empowered, will strike the Dauphin
The old wooden ball will roll about
Going beyond the Duke's instructions.

The traditional interpretation depends on Nostradamus intending 'De bois' as an ill-disguised code for the priest Guillaume Dubois (1656–1723) who rose to be first minister of France under the Regency of the Duke of Orléans in 1722. Dubois had charge of the young King Louis XV's spiritual welfare, and Nostradamus forecasts that he will fail in this duty, submitting the young king to more discipline than the Duke would ordain. The reference to the old wooden ball may well be a pun on Dubois' ability to survive the ebb and flow of the political tides.

1727

Le tiers climat sous Aries comprins,
L'an mil sept cens vingt et sept en Octobre
Le Roy de Perse par ceux d'Egypte prins,
Conflit, mort, perte: à la croix grand approbre.

The third climate will be under Aries
In October, of the year 1727
The Persian king will be taken by the Egyptians
Battle, death and losses: the cross will be excoriated.

This is extraordinarily specific, with Nostradamus giving the actual year and month of an event that took place 161 years after his death. In October 1727, a peace was indeed arranged between the Turks and the Persians. As a result, Ottoman influence was consolidated throughout the region, to the detriment of the Christian powers.

1736

Saturn: au beuf joue en l'eau, Mars en fleiche
Six de Fevrier mortalité donra
Ceux de Tardaigne à Briges si grand breche
Qu'à Ponteroso chef Barbarin mourra,

Saturn: Taurus plays in Aquarius, Mars in Sagittarius
The sixth day of February brings death
The Sardinians will make such a big breach at Bruges
That the barbarian chief will die at Ponteroso.

Astrologers have not arrived at a satisfactory future date based
on this seemingly specific celestial pattern, but one claim is that
this heavenly configuration pertained in 1736. On 6 February of
that year, the most notable event was the landing of John Wesley,
the founder of Methodism, in America – where he received a
distinctly hostile reception from the Georgia colonists, but did
not lose his life.

⧖ 1736 ⧖

Au fort chasteau de Viglanne et Resviers
Sera serré le puisnay de Nancy
Dedans Turin seront ards les premiers
Lors que de dueil Lyon sera transi.

At the fortress of Viglanne and Resviers
They will imprison the youngest born of Nancy
The leading citizens of Turin will be burned
When Lyons is transported with grief.

There are several clues in this verse. The most interesting is Nancy, the former capital of the province of Lorraine. Here Stanislas Leczinski, last Duke of Lorraine, who abdicated the Polish throne in 1736 and was given Lorraine by his son-in-law Louis XV of France, established one of the most beautiful cities in Europe. The reference to burning in line 3 (though referring, inexplicably, to Turin) is also interesting, because Stanislas died from burns received in an accident in 1766, at the age of eighty-nine.

Le successeur de la Duché viendra
Beaucoup plus outre que la mer de Tosquane
Gauloise branche la Florence tiendra
Dans son giron d'accord nautique Rane.

The heir to the Duchy will come
From far beyond the sea of Tuscany
A French branch will hold Florence
In his lap will be a naval agreement with the frog.

This is a remarkably sharp insight into the future of Florence, which passed from Medici possession into that of Francis, Duke of Lorraine, in 1737.

1743

La pille faite à la coste marine
La cita nova et parents amenez
Plusieurs de Malte par le fait de Messine
Estroit serrez seront mal guardonnez.

Pillage occurs on the sea coast
Family relations are favoured in the new city
Some Maltese, because of Messina's acts
Will be locked up, and poorly rewarded.

The island of Malta is situated in the Mediterranean, below Sicily. Messina separates the north-western corner of Sicily from mainland Italy. In 1743 Messina was decimated by a plague. Any merchants passing through the straits of Messina from Malta would have been forcibly quarantined to prevent the spread of the pestilence, thus ensuring that they were poorly rewarded for their pains.

1745

Soubs le terroir du rond globe lunaire,
Lors que sera dominateur Mercure,
L'isle d'Escosse fera un luminaire,
Qui les Anglais mettra à déconfiture.

On this world beneath the moon
While Mercury is in the ascendant
The isle of Scotland will produce a leader
Who will cause the English discomfort.

Prince Charles, the 'Young Pretender' intent on regaining the crowns of Scotland and England for the Stuart dynasty dispossessed of it in 1588, landed in Inverness, Scotland in 1745. He collected together an army of highlanders and succeeded in seizing Edinburgh, proclaiming himself king. He marched south as far as Derby before the series of reverses that were to culminate in the carnage at Culloden on 16 April 1746.

Un Empereur naistra pres d'Italie
Qui a l'Empire sera vendu bien cher
Diront avec quels gens il se ralie,
Qu'on trouvera moins prince que boucher.

An Emperor will be born near Italy
Who will cost the Empire dearly
Judged by the people who surround him
He will be considered less Prince, than butcher.

Napoleon was born 'near Italy', in 1769, on the island of Corsica. It can be argued that he cost the French Empire dearly, both in terms of life and prestige. In English popular newspapers of the time, Napoleon was known as the 'French Butcher', a reference both to his humble birth and military tactics.

D'un nom farouche tel proferé sera,
Que les trois soeurs aurant fato le nom
Puis grand peuple par langue et faict dira
Plus que nul autre bruit et renom.

He will be known by a savage name
The name is the destiny of three sisters.
He will address a great people in words and actions
His fame and renown greater than any other.

A new Messiah? Possibly, but more likely Napoleon Bonaparte
(1769–1821). The name Napoleon is a savage one, deriving from
the Greek word for destroyer – and Bonaparte's campaigns
destroyed more lives, including one and a half million French
ones, than any previous conflict in history. He was a great orator
and legislator as well as soldier. He had three sisters, Elisa,
Pauline and Caroline, who each benefited from their brother's
eager desire to make the Bonapartes the first family of Europe.

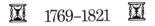

1769–1821

Du nom qui onques ne fut au Roy Gaulois,
Jamais ne fut un fouldre si craintif
Tremblant l'Italie, l'Espaigne et les Anglois,
De femme estrangiers grandement attentif.

From a name never held by French kings
Comes a fear-inducing thunderbolt
Italy, Spain and the English tremble
He will be drawn to foreign women.

The king who was not a king has to be Napoleon Bonaparte, whose name had never before ranked among the rulers of France. Lines 2 and 3 are self-evident, and Napoleon's proclivity for foreign-born women is also well documented: Josephine, his first wife, was a Creole, born in Haiti; his mistress, Guiseppina Grassini, was Italian; another mistress, Maria Walewska, who bore him an illegitimate child, was Polish.

⧗ 1774 ⧗

Pluys, faim, guerre, en Perse non cesée,
La foy trop grande trahira le Monarque,
Par la finie en Gaule commencée,
Secret augure pour a un estre parque.

Rain, hunger, unceasing war in the east
His excess of faith will betray the monarch
It's the beginning of the end for France
A secret augury for one who lives apart.

King Louis XVI of France succeeded his grandfather, Louis XV, in 1774 aged twenty. The kingdom was bankrupt through prolonged war and endemic corruption. Louis' reign was marked by a series of poor harvests, mass starvation and unjust burdens of taxation imposed on all classes except the aristocracy. The king, remote from his people and ill-served by his advisors, must indeed have had premonitions of his country's and his own fate in the looming Revolution.

Istra du Mont Gaulfier et Aventin,
Qui par trou avertira l'armée
Entre deux rocs sera prins le butin,
De S E X T. mansol faillir le renommee.

From Montgaulfier and Aventin will go forth
One who, through a hole, will warn the army
The booty will be taken from between two rocks
The renown of Sextus the celibate will diminish.

This quatrain appears to foretell, even down to their names, the invention of the hot air balloon by the Montgolfier brothers, in 1783. The balloon was immediately used to scout enemy positions at the Battle of Fleurus in 1794. This victory then led, by a circuitous route, to Napoleon's sack of Rome, indicated by the booty being taken between two rocks. Pius VI ('sextus') was captured by Napoleon, and his influence and renown were indeed diminished by the Treaty of Tolentino, in 1797.

 1789

De gent esclave chansons, chants et requestes,
Captifs par Princes et Seigneur aux prisons
A l'avenir par idiots sans testes,
Seront reçus par divines oraisons.

Songs, chants and demands will come from the
  enslaved
Held captive by the nobility in their prisons
At a later date, brainless idiots
Will take these as divine utterances.

The French Revolution was caused by social unrest, stemming from the power of the aristocracy and their abuse of it. The Paris mob, thinking themselves liberated, howled and chanted outside the walls of Louis XVI's prison. Men like Danton (1759–1794) and Robespierre (1758–1794) took these cries quite literally to heart, a mistake which cost them their own heads on the guillotine.

1789

Faux esposer viendra topographie,
Seront les cruches des monuments ouvertes
Pulluler secte saincte philosophie,
Pour blanches, noirs, et pour antiques verts.

He will come to expose the false topography
The monumental urns will be opened
Sects, and sacred texts will thrive
Black instead of white, new for old.

Following the National Assembly of 22 December 1789, everything
changed in France. The funeral urns of the French Kings were
destroyed and their ashes scattered. Even the Church was
abolished, to be replaced by the cult of Reason.

En bref seront de retour sacrifices,
Contrevenans seront mis a martyre,
Plus ne seront moins, abbez ne novices
Le miel sera beaucoup plus cher que cire.

Briefly sacrifices will be made again
Protesters will be martyred
No more monks, abbots or novices
Honey will be costlier than candles.

The murderous destruction of the English monasteries in 1536, ordered by Henry VIII in his unilateral Reformation, will have been in Nostradamus's mind as he predicted a similar fate for France's abbeys. The Church in France hung on to its influence and its vast wealth right up to the Revolution – longer, perhaps than the seer expected. Priests were murdered (judicially or otherwise) in vast numbers. Most of the land and property was seized by the moneyed 'notables' of the Revolution – and remains in the hands of their heirs today.

⌛ 1789–93 ⌛

Le tiers premier pis que ne fait Neron,
Vuidez vaillant que sang humain respandre
R'edifier sera le fornoron,
Siecle d'or, mort, nouveau roi grand esclandre.

The first of the third behaves worse than Nero
Go, brave one, that human blood may flow
The oven will be rebuilt
Golden century, dead, a new king and a great scandal.

The first of the third is the Tiers Etat, precursor of the French Revolution in 1789. The blood-letting it engendered would be far worse even than Nero's. The guillotine was placed in the Place de la Revolution, where before there had only been kilns (ovens) for baking tiles. The golden century refers to the reign of the three Louis, XIV, XV and XVI. The scandal is the beheading of Louis XVI.

Changer à Beaune, Nuy, Chalons et Dijon,
Le duc voulant amander la Barrée
Marchant pres fleuve, poisson, bec de plongeon,
Vers la queue; porte sera serrée.

Changes to Beaune, Nuits, Chalon and Dijon
The king wishes to improve the lot of the Carmelites
Merchants near the rivers; fish; the beaks of diving birds
Towards the end the gates will be shut.

The Carmelites, an order of nuns whose silent and contemplative lives consisted of prayer, penance and hard work, were forcibly deprived of their nunneries during the French Revolution of 1789–99.

⌛ 1789–99 ⌛

D'esprit de regne munismes descriées,
Et seront peuples esmuez contre leur Roi
Paix, faict nouveau, sainctes loix empirées,
Rapis onc fut en si tres dur arroi.

The spirit of the kingdom undermines its defences
People will rise against the king
A new peace is made, holy laws deteriorate
Paris has never before found herself in such dire straits.

This applies to the French Revolution of 1789–99, in which the
people rose against King Louis XVI (1754–1793) and his wife,
Marie Antoinette (1755–1793), causing them both to be be-
headed. During this terrible period the Catholic Church was
almost completely undermined, many churches being either
sacked or destroyed. Paris continued in dire straits until
Napoleon Bonaparte's election as commander of the Army of
the Interior in 1794, in gratitude for his saving of the Tuileries
Palace.

Plainctes et pleurs cris et grands urlemens
Pres de Narbon à Bayonne et en Foix
O quel horrible calamitz changemens
Avant que Mars revolu quelques fois.

Laments and howls and terrible cries
Near Narbonne, at Bayonne and in Foix
Oh what horrible calamities and changes occur
Before Mars has made several revolutions.

Mars revolves around the earth once every 687 days. The horrors of the French Revolution lasted for the space of five Martian circuits, and culminated in the election of Napoleon, on 19 November 1799, as First Consul of France.

1790

Foudre en Bourgongne fera cas portenteux,
Que par engin oncques ne pourrait faire,
De leur senat sacriste fait boiteux
Fera scavoir aux ennemis l'affaire.

Lightning in Burgundy will portend more
Than could ever have been suggested by trickery
From their hidden councils, a lame priest
Will make known the truth to their enemies.

Charles de Talleyrand-Périgord (1754–1838) was the consummate diplomat. Crippled as a child in a fall, he gave up his position as Bishop of Antin in 1790 to join the Revolutionaries. He became a supporter of Napoleon, but was later instrumental in having the Bourbons returned to office, exhibiting, during his long and fascinating life, the *volte-face* capacities of a latter-day Janus.

⌛ 1790 ⌛

Yeux clos ouverts d'antique fantasie
L'habit des seules seront mis a néant;
Le grand monarque chastira leur frenaisie,
Ravir des temples le thrésor par devant.

Eyes closed to truth but open to ancient paganism
The priesthood will be reduced to nothing
Le grand monarch will punish their frenzy
Stripping the temples of their treasure.

Nostradamus looks fearfully ahead to the ravishing of the French church in the Revolution. The grand monarch is Louis XVI, who was forced on 22 July 1790 to issue the Civil Constitution of the Clergy, under which church property was nationalised and priests became employees of the state.

Dans Avignon tout le Chef de l'empire
Fera arest pour Paris desolé
Tricast tiendra l'Annibalique ire,
Lyon par change sera mel consolé.

The empire's supreme chief will stop at Avignon
Because Paris is deserted
The three towers will contain African anger
The lion, on the other hand, will be consoled by honey.

Avignon ceased to belong to the Vatican in 1791, a time when
Paris no longer even paid lip-service to the Catholic Church.
Large parts of Africa, however, were later evangelised, containing
her potential power and Europeanising her. The Protestant
British lion, master of most of what remained of the continent,
was secularly consoled by possession of the honey of world trade.

⌛ 1791 ⌛

De nuict viendra par la forest de Reines,
Deux pars, vaultorte, Herne la pierre blanche,
Le moyne noir en gris dedans Varennes:
Esleu Cap. cause tempeste, feu, sang, tranche.

By night through the forest of Reines will come
The couple, via a circuitous route, Herne the white stone
The black monk in grey towards Varennes:
The elected Capet, causing storm, fire, blood, cut.

The flight of Louis XVI and Marie-Antoinette, from Paris,
through the forest at night, ending in arrest at Varennes on 21
June 1791. *Herne* is an anagram for Reine and *la pierre blanche*
refers to the fact that on the day the queen was dressed in white.
The black monk is the king, disguised in grey on the day. The
elected Capet also refers to the king, for under France's
Revolutionary Constituent Assembly, Louis had lately been
'elected' head of a state destined for war and regicide.

⧖ 1792 ⧖

Le part solus mari sera mitré,
Retour conflict passera sur le thuille
Par cinq cens un trahir sera tiltré,
Narbon et Saulce par conteuax avons d'huile.

The lonely, separated husband will be forcibly hatted
On his return, there will be conflict at the Tuileries
Of the five hundred, one traitor will be ennobled
Narbon and Saluces will have oil for their blades.

When Louis and Marie Antoinette fled from their detention in
Paris, they were stopped at Varennes (actually named in another
quatrain). That night they stayed in a Monsieur Saluces' house.
On his return to Paris on 20 June 1792, Louis was separated from
his family and humiliated, in the Tuileries, by being forcibly
hatted with a revolutionary cap by a mob of five hundred in
August 1792. A moderate called Narbon later tried to persuade
the Council to pardon Louis, but to no avail.

⧗ 1792 ⧗

Aupres du lac Leman sera conduite
Par garse estrange cité voulant trahir
Avant son meurtre à Auspourg la grande suitte
Et ceux du Rhin la viendront invahir.

He will be led to near Lake Geneva
By a foreign minx who wants to betray the city
Before her murder a great throng will enter Augsburg
The Rhinelanders will come to invade it.

Marie Antoinette, about whom Nostradamus often speaks in
unflattering terms, was the daughter of the Empress Maria
Theresa of Austria. Aware of her imminent fate in 1792, Austria
and her allies threatened dire retribution against France. But
she was executed just the same, in October 1793, and Austrian
invaders, among others, were repelled from France by revolutionary armies.

La pitié grande sera sans loing tarder
Ceux qui donoient seront contrains de prendre
Nudz affamez de froit, soif, soi bander
Les monts passer commettant grand esclandre.

The terrible event won't be long in coming
Those who gave will now be forced to take
Naked, starving, cold and thirsty, they will band together
To cross the mountains causing great outrage.

Widely held to be a foretelling of the dissolution of the French established church during the Revolution. Thousands of churches were desecrated and hundreds of priests murdered, with or without trial. Many members of the clergy, utterly dispossessed, fled to Italy in the hope of protection from the church of Rome. Europe was scandalised by this ill-treatment of priests.

La Royne Ergaste voyant sa fille blesme
Par un regret dans l'estomach enclos,
Cris lamentables seront lors d'Angolesme,
Et au germain mariage forclos.

The imprisoned Queen seeing her wan daughter
By a regret in the closed stomach
There will be lamenting cries at Angoulême
And a marriage to a first cousin.

The captive Queen is Marie Antoinette, imprisoned in the Temple with her husband Louis XVI and their two children. Her daughter, Marie Thérèse Charlotte, wan because of her family's unhappy predicament, is aged fourteen, but has been betrothed since she was nine to her first cousin, the Duke of Angoulême. Marie Thérèse, known to history as 'the orphan of the Temple', survived and the wedding took place in 1799. The closed stomach must allude to the sad fact that the marriage was childless.

⏳ 1793 ⏳

Le charbon blanc du noir sera chassé,
Prisonnier faicte mené au tomberreau
More Chameau sus piedz entrelassez,
Lors le puismé sillera l'aubereau.

The white coal is driven out by the black
He is made a prisoner, taken to the tumbril
The rogue's feet are tied, as is the custom
The youngest will let slip the falcon.

The first line consists of wordplay identifying the Bourbon king, Louis XVI (1754–1793). Imprisoned in the Temple and later condemned to death by the Convention, who voted 683 to 38 in favour of Madame Guillotine, Louis was forced into a tumbril by the revolutionary guards, where his feet were tied. He was executed later that day, 21 January, in the Place de la Revolution.

1793

Le regne prins le Roi conviera,
La dame prinse a mort jurez a sort,
La vie a Royne fils on desniera,
Et la pillex au fort de la consort.

The King will acknowledge his realm is taken
The Queen is taken to a death ordained by a jury
Which will deny her son his life
And the prostitute goes the same way as the consort.

It looks an accurate depiction of the fate of Louis XVI at the hands of the Commune in October 1793, along with Marie-Antoinette. The Dauphin was spared the Guillotine, but indeed denied his life. The prostitute could very well be the renowned mistress of Louis XV, Madame du Barry, who went to the block in the same year.

Barbare empire par le tiers usurpé,
La plus grand part de son sang mettra à mort,
Par mort senile, par luy le quart frappé,
Pour peur que sang par le sang ne soit mort.

The barbarous state, usurped by the third party
Will put to death many people of its own blood
An old man's death will hurt the fourth party
For fear that blood will not wish to die by blood.

Robespierre's French Revolutionary Reign of Terror, in which at least 25,000 citizens went to the guillotine, inspires this curious quatrain. The third party refers to Robespierre himself. The identities of the old man and the fourth party remain uncertain.

Par grand discord la trombe tremblera
Accord rompu dressant la teste au ciel
Bouche sanglante dans le sang nagera,
Au sol la face ointe de laict et miel.

The horn sounds discordantly
Following a broken vow, he raises his head to the sky
His blood-stained mouth awash with blood
His fallen face is anointed with milk and honey.

The execution of Louis XVI on the 21 January 1793. Following his broken vow not to attempt escape from Paris, the trumpets sounded ironically as he ascended the steps of the guillotine. Reciting the third verse of the third psalm, *exaltus capum meum* (Lord, I lift my face to heaven), Sanson, his executioner, triggered Madame Guillotine, then raised the king's head, quite literally, on high. It has been well-documented that severed heads bleed from the mouth. The fallen king's face had been anointed with milk and honey nineteen years before, during his coronation.

Des principaux de cité rebellee
Qui tiendront fort pour liberté ravoir
Detrencher masles, infelice meslee,
Cris hurlemens à Nantes piteux voir.

The leading citizens of the rebellious city
Will struggle hard to regain their liberty
The men will be torn apart, a sad mess
The cries and howls at Nantes will be piteous to see.

The horrors of the *Noyades* at Nantes took place in 1793, a time of terrible excesses in the French Revolution. A thousand eminent Nantais citizens were guillotined for resisting the National Convention, and hundreds more, men and women, priests and nuns, were tied naked together on barges in the middle of the Loire river, which were then sunk.

Prince de beauté tant venuste,
Au chef menee, le second faict trahi
La cité au glaive de poudre face aduste,
Par le trop grand meurte le chef du Roi hai.

The beautiful prince, so handsome
Taken to the leader, he betrays the second deed
The city is put to the sword, its facade burnt by gunpowder
The king's head is spited, for too much murdering.

Louis XVI (1774–1792) was considered beautiful in his youth. Forced to agree that the monarchy should become purely constitutional, he betrayed his oath by fleeing to Varennes as part of a misguided counter-revolution. Guillotined in 1793, his head was spited (ridiculed) in front of the crowd, then thrown into a quick-lime pit.

⧗ 1793 ⧗

De la cité marine et tributaire,
La teste raze prendra la satrapie
Chasser sordide qui puis sera contraire
Par quatorze ans tiendra la tyrannie.

From the marine and tributary city
The crop-head will take up the government
He will chase his evil opponent
The tyranny will last for fourteen years.

Napoleon retook Toulon from the English in 1793. He later shaved off his revolutionary locks and adopted a hairstyle that resembled his idol, Julius Caesar. The evil opponent in line 3 may refer to General Moreau, Napoleon's chief rival, who later offered his services to the Allied Coalitions fighting for the Bourbon restoration. Napoleon enjoyed absolute power for fourteen years, from 9 November 1793 to 13 April 1814.

🕰 1793 🕰

Dans deux logis de nuict le feu prendra
Plusieurs dedans estouffes et rostis
Pres de deux fleuves pour seul il adviendra
Sol, l'Arq et Caper tous seront amortis.

Fire will engulf two houses at night
Several within are suffocated and burnt
It will certainly happen near two rivers
When the Sun, Sagittarius and Capricorn are transited.

Girondists allied with Royalists seized power in Lyons in
1793 but were burned out by an army of the revolutionary
Convention. Lyons is a very important city to Nostradamus, as
it was here, at the confluence of the Rhône and Saône rivers,
that Pope Clement V was crowned in 1305.

A soubstenir la grand cappe troublee,
Pour l'esclaircir les rouges marcheront,
De mort famille sera presque accablee.
Les rouges rouges le rouge assomeront.

To support the great, troubled cappe
The reds will march to clarify it
A family nearly overcome by death
The bloody reds will strike the red one down.

Cappe signifies Capulet, a family name of the French Royal line at the time of the French Revolution. Despite the support of the more moderate Girondins, all the surviving family, bar one, died under the guillotine. A year later, Maximilien Robespierre (1758–1794), the red one, who had led the paradoxically-named Committee of Public Safety during the terrible months between April 1793 and July 1794, was himself executed.

 1795

Avant venu de ruine Celtique
Dedans le temple deux parlementeront
Poignard coeur, d'un monté au coursier et pique
Sans faire bruit le grand enterreront.

Before the ruin of France
Two will parley inside the temple
Stabbed in the heart by a mounted knight
They will bury the great one in secret.

The temple is taken to be the Temple in Paris where King Louis XVI and his family were confined in 1792 during the French Revolution. The Dauphin, heir to Louis and thus Louis XVII on his father's execution in 1793, died some time soon after of unknown causes. News of his death was made official in 1795 and his body was never discovered.

1795

Le grand credit d'or, d'argent l'abondance
Fera aveugler par libide honneur
Sera cogneu d'adultere l'offense,
Qui parviendra à son grand deshonneur.

So much gold and silver
Will blind honour, through lust
The adulteress's offence will become known
Causing her great dishonour.

The geographical boundaries of the present day United States were created on the back of an unstoppable land and gold-lust, at the expense of some three hundred native tribes. Beginning with the Treaty of Greenville in 1795, the offences perpetrated in the name of the adulteress (the Statue of Liberty) have only recently been acknowledged, somewhat tarnishing US claims to be the 'land of the free'.

Terre Italique pres des monts tremblera,
Lyon et coq non trop confederez
En lieu de peur l'un l'autre s'aidera,
Seul Catulon et Celtes moderez.

Alpine Italy will tremble
Cock and lion will be disunited
In a place of fear, one will help the other
Only liberty will moderate the French.

Napoleon began his Italian campaign in 1795, for ever changing the face of Italy. The French cock and the English lion were consequently thrown into open conflict. At Waterloo, the Prussians helped the English, liberating France from Napoleon's stranglehold, and Europe from tyranny.

🜨 1796 🜨

Au grand Empire par viendra tout un autre,
Bonté distant plus de felicité;
Régi par un issu non loing du peautre
Corruer Regnes grand infelicté.

To the great Empire will come a very different man
Far from kindness and ever farther from happiness
Ruled by one from whose bed he has just risen
To bring the Kingdom great unhappiness.

Widely believed to refer to the influence exerted on Napoleon
Bonaparte by Joséphine de Beauharnais (1763–1814), whom he
married in 1796. Napoleon had their marriage dissolved in 1809
for lack of any surviving children.

⌛ 1796 ⌛

Au profligez de paix les ennemis
Apres avoir l'Italie superee
Noir sanguinaire, rouge sera commis
Feu, sang verser, eaue de sang couloree.

The enemies of those weakened by peace
Having already overcome Italy
Red deeds will be done by the bloody black being
Fire, spilled blood, blood-stained water.

It is important to bear in mind the affection Nostradamus felt
for Italy, where he travelled widely as an itinerant physician.
He often speaks in fearful tones about the country's future,
and quite blithely refers to it as *Italie*, even though its
unification under that name was more than three hundred
years off in the future. Here, he is using 'red' in the late
eighteenth century context of revolution, and looking ahead
to 1796, when Napoleon Bonaparte was appointed to lead
France's revolutionary army in Italy.

Avant l'assaut l'oraison prononcee,
Milan prins d'aigle par embusches decevez
Muraille antique par canons enfoncee,
Par feu et sang à mercy peu receus.

A speech is delivered before the assault
Milan is ambushed and captured by the eagle
Ancient walls are breached by cannon
In the ensuing fire and bloodshed, few receive quarter.

Napoleon took Milan twice, on 15 May 1796, then again on 2 June 1800, each time allowing his soldiers to sack the city. He made a famous speech before the first assault, in which he promised his men glory and booty in profusion if they followed him. History records that they did, and obtained both.

Tout à l'entour de la grand Cité,
Seront soldats logez par champs et villes
Donner assaut Paris, Rome incité,
Sur le pont lors sera faicte grande pille.

All around the great city
Soldiers will be garrisoned in the fields and towns
Paris will make the assault, Rome incited
The Pope will be subjected to many depredations.

The sad history of Rome, between 1797 and 1809, incorporates two sackings by France and the relinquishment of part of the Papal States by Pope Pius VI. It was followed, twelve years later, by a total capitulation under his successor, Pius VII, the States being incorporated into Napoleon's nascent French Empire.

Saturne et Mars en Leo Espagne captive,
Par chef Libique au Conflit attrape;
Proche de Malte, Herodde prinse vive,
Et Romain sceptre sera par Coq frappé.

With Saturn and Mars in Leo, Spain is captive
By a Libyan chief taken in battle
At Malta Rhodes heroes are quickly taken
And the Roman sceptre is struck by the Cock.

Napoleon occupied the island of Malta in 1798, seizing it with little resistance from the Knights of Rhodes.

Si France passes outre mer Lygustique,
Tu le verras en isles et mers enclos,
Mahomet contraire, plus mer Hadriatique,
Chevaux et d'asnes tu rangeras les os.

France, if you go beyond the Lygustian sea
You will see yourself trapped in islands and seas
Mohammed will oppose you, more in the Adriatic
You will be gnawing the bones of horses and mules.

A warning to Napoleon Bonaparte lest he extend himself too far
(beyond the Lygustian sea – the Gulf of Genoa) to invade Egypt.
On islands including Malta, as well as at Alexandria, French
forces were starved under siege by Mohammed in the shape of
the Turks, while in the Adriatic they faced the British fleet, later
that year to wreck the French fleet in Aboukir Bay.

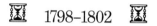

Dans la Sardaigne un noble Roi viendra
Que ne tiendra que trois ans la royaume,
Plusieurs couleurs avec soi conjoindra,
Lui mesmes apres soin someil marrit scome.

A noble king will come to Sardinia
Who will only reign for three years
Many colours will join him
After sleeping, he will be taunted.

There were no kings of Sardinia until the eighteenth century, when King Charles Emmanuel IV retired there. He reigned for three years, from 1798–1802. On his abdication in favour of his brother, Victor Emmanuel I, he retired, humiliated, to Rome, where, no doubt in desperation, he became a Jesuit. He died there in 1819.

1799

Romain Pontife garde de t'approcher
De la cité que deux fleuves arrouse.
Ton sang viendra auprès de là cracher,
Toy et les tiens quand fleurira la rose.

Roman Pontiff, take care of approaching
The city irrigated by two rivers
Your blood will come close to the spitting
You and yours when the rose comes into bloom.

Pope Pius VI (1717–99) is warned to avoid the city at the
confluence of the rivers Rhône and Saône, namely Lyon. It was
good advice, which the Pontiff did not take. He died at Valence,
close by, in August 1799, of a violent coughing fit. He had been
taken there, as a captive, by the French forces who had seized
Rome in the previous year on the pretext Pius had ordered the
murder of a member of the French embassy.

1799

Les citoyens de Mesopotamie
Yrés encontre amis de Tarraconne
Jeux, ritz, banquetz, toute gent endormie
Vicaire au Rosne, prins cité, ceux d'Ausone.

The citizens of Mesopotamia
Are angry with their friends from Tarragona
Games, rites, banquets, everyone asleep
The Pope near the Rhone; the city, and the Italians, taken.

Mesopotamia is Nostradamian code for a land between two rivers (the Tigris and Euphrates of biblical Mesopotamia). In this case it may well mean that part of southern France encompassed by the Rhône and Saône rivers. The allusion here is to Pope Pius VI's detention during the French advance into Italy of 1799.

 1799

Par Mars contraire sera la monarchie,
Du grand pecheur en trouble ruineux
Jeune noir rouge prendra la hierarchie,
Les prorditeurs iront jour bruineux.

Mars will adversely influence the monarchy
The Pope will be in terrible trouble
The young red king will take over
The traitors will choose a misty day to act.

Revolutionary Mars, the God of War, overthrows the Bourbon monarchy and threatens the stability of the Catholic Church. In 1799, Napoleon, the young red king, chooses the month of mists, Brumaire, to engage in his *coup d'état*. As a result, Pope Pius VI is imprisoned, and later dies, in Valence. An altogether remarkable quatrain.

Predictions of Nostradamus for the
17th CENTURY

La deschassee au regne tournera,
Ses ennemis trouvés des conjurés
Plus que jamais son temps triomphera,
Trois et septante à mort trop asseures.

She who is driven from the kingdom, will return
Her enemies are found among the conspirators
More than ever her era will be triumphant
Three and seventy she dies.

Elizabeth I of England (1533–1603) was imprisoned, exiled and plotted against in the years preceding her accession to the throne in 1558. She later antagonised her Catholic subjects by reverting to Protestantism, and was bedevilled by Popish plots during the entire course of her reign. She presided over one of the greatest ever flowerings of English art, culture and music, and died in 1603, in her seventieth year.

La grand Bretagne comprinse l'Angleterre,
Viendra par eaux si haut à inonder
La ligue neufue d'Ausonne fera guerre,
Que contre eux ils se viendront bander.

Great Britain, including England
Will be covered by deep floods
The new Ausonne league will make war against her
So that her various parts will band together.

In Nostradamus's time, England, Scotland and Wales were not united into the one kingdom of Great Britain. This process only began under James I, who formally assumed the title of King of Great Britain on 24 October 1604. The floods in this quatrain are probably those which occurred in January 1607, when water covered the Somerset levels for thirty miles in every direction.

Montera haut sur le bien plus à dextre
Demourra assis sur la pierre quarree
Vers le midi posé à la fenestre
Baston tortu en main, bouche serree.

He will rise high over the one to the right of him
He will retain the squared seat
Towards midday, at the window
His mouth pursed, he will hold a crooked staff.

Cardinal Richelieu (1585–1642) began his vertiginous rise to power in France by being consecrated a bishop (thus the crooked staff) in 1607, aged only twenty-two. As chief minister to King Louis XIII from 1629, Richelieu was the *de facto* ruler of France. Thus did he rise above the one to the right of him.

Clergé Romain l'an mil six cens et neuf
Au chef de l'an feras election
D'un gris et noir de la Compagne
Qui onc ne feut si maling.

The Roman Clergy, in 1609
Will have a New Year's election
A grey and black one from Campania
Never was there a wickeder man.

Perhaps due to the rare specific date, this quatrain can be seen as a failure. However it certainly could have occurred had not Pope Paul V, who reigned from 1605 to 1621, recovered from the serious illness he underwent that year, amidst the frenetic intrigues of his entourage to arrange for a possible successor.

1610

Serpens transmis dans la caige de fer,
Ou les enfans septaines du Roy sont pris
Les vieux et peres sortiront bas de l'enfer,
Ains mourir voir de fruict mort et cris.

A coffin is placed in the iron vault
Where the seven children of the king are held
Their forebears will arise from the pit of hell
Lamenting the death of their line.

Following his correct prediction of the death of Henri II (1519–1559) in a joust, Nostradamus foretells the fall of the entire House of Valois. Henri's seven children by Catherine de Medici (1519–1589) all came to unhappy ends, the women in childbirth, the men through premature illness or murder.

Norvege et Dace, et l'isle Britannique,
Pars les unis frères seront vexées;
Le chef Romain issue du sang Gallique.
Et les copies aux foret repoulsées.

Norway and Dacia, and the British Isles
Will be angered by the united brothers
The Roman chief, of French blood
And his forces driven back to the forest.

The Thirty Years War in Europe broke out in Prague in 1618. 'Norway' signifies the Scandinavian armies who intervened in the war on the Protestant side against the forces of the Holy Roman Emperor Ferdinand II. Dacia is the ancient name for the region of central Europe now mostly occupied by Romania, but then a battlefield between Protestant and Catholic interests. Britain's role in the war was as a frustrated mediator, and a notable supplier of mercenaries to both sides.

1618

Secteur de Sectes, grand paine au delateur,
Beste en theatre, dresse le jeu scenique,
Du fait inique ennobli l'inventeur,
Par sectes, monde confus et schismatique.

The arch sectarian who lives by his whispers
The theatrical clown sets up the comic scene
This wicked notion will elevate its inventor
The world will be confused and divided by sects.

Nostradamus excoriates Martin Luther (1483–1546) whose Reformation brought the Protestant and Catholic sects of Europe into such destructive conflict in the Thirty Years War of 1618–48.

Par grand fureur le Roi Romain Belgique
Vexer vouldra par phalange barbare
Fureur grinsseant chassera gent Libyque
Despuis Pannons jusques Hercules la hare.

In a great fury the Roman king will come
With a foreign horde, to vex Belgium
Gnashing his teeth, he will chase the Libyans
From Hungary to Gibraltar.

The Thirty Years War from 1618–48 was the most devastating of all European conflicts up to that time. The Roman king was the Austrian Archduke Ferdinand of Bohemia (1578–1637), soon to become King Ferdinand II of Hungary and then Holy Roman Emperor, who sought to chase Protestant heretics ('Libyans') out of his domains.

🏛 1620 🏛

La terre et l'air gelleront si grand eau
Lorsqu'on viendra pour jeudi venerer
Ce qui sera jamais ne feut si beau
Des quatre pars le viendront honnorer.

The earth and the air will freeze such an expanse of water
When Thursday becomes a day of prayer
That which will be was never so beautiful
From all four corners they will come to venerate him.

The day of prayer on Thursday refers to Thanksgiving Day, held on the fourth Thursday in November in the US. In the cold winter of 1620, the Pilgrim Fathers lost half of their entire complement of 103 men, women and children. The remainder survived thanks to the local Indian tribe, with whom they allegedly sat down to dinner, instigating the present custom of inviting guests to share in the Thanksgiving feast.

1624

Celui qu'estoit bien avant dans le regne
Ayant chef rouge proche à la hierarchie
Aspre et cruel, et se fera tant craindre
Succedera à sacré monarchie.

He who was ahead in the reigning stakes
Having a red leader near the seat of power
Harsh and cruel, he will make himself so feared
That he will succeed to the sacred monarchy.

The red leader near the seat of power can only be Cardinal Richelieu (1585–1642), the ruthless statesman who became Minister of State to Louis XIII of France in 1624. Nostradamus seems to anticipate Richelieu's elevation to the Papacy, but the Cardinal took a different direction – later becoming *de facto* ruler of France.

Le Prins hors de son terroir Celtique
Sera trahi, deceu par l'interprete
Rouan, Rochelle par ceux de l'Armorique
Au port de blaue deceus par moine et prebstre.

The Prince, outside his French territory
Will be betrayed, deceived by the interpreter
Rouen, La Rochelle, by those of Brittany
Deceived by monks and priests at the port of Blaye.

This seems to be concerned with the suppression of the
Huguenots (notably by Cardinal Richelieu at La Rochelle in
1628). The Prince would be Louis XIII under the regency of
Marie de Medici, whom Richelieu served as a special adviser.
Richelieu made a treaty with the English and arranged the
marriage in 1625 of Henrietta Maria, Louis' sister, to Charles I –
a union with a Protestant king which many in France would
have regarded as a betrayal of the Catholic faith.

1627

De l'acqueduct d'Uticense, Gardoing,
Par la forest et mont inaccessible,
En mi du pont sera tasché au poing,
Le chef nemans et qui tant sera terrible.

Crossing the Gard, by the aqueduct of Uzés
Through forest and inaccessible mountain
He will cut a stanchion, halfway across the bridge
Becoming the chief at Nîmes, and very terrible.

A reference to the Roman aqueduct that once connected Uzès to
Nîmes. In 1627 the Duke of Rohan rode to the aid of his fellow
Calvinists, besieged at Nîmes. He moved his artillery by means
of the aqueduct, thus avoiding the heavy forest and inaccessible
mountains of line 2. Line 3 refers to Rohan's soldiers cutting
some of the stanchions of the bridge over the Gard to allow the
cannon to be brought forward. When Rohan arrived at Nîmes,
he was put in command of the garrison.

1628

Siège à cité et de nuit assaillé,
Peu eschapez non loing de Mer conflict
Femme de joys, retour fils, defaillie
Poison et lettres cachées dans le plic.

The city besieged and attacked at night
A few escape the battle, not far from the sea
A woman faint with joy at her son's return
Poison is hidden in the folds of the letters.

The city is La Rochelle, the Huguenot stronghold on the Poitou coast ruthlessly besieged by Cardinal Richelieu (1585–1642) in 1628. The identity of the mother and son, with its flavour of intrigue, is in doubt, but Queen Marie de Medici, mother of Louis XIII, whom the Cardinal served as minister, loathed Richelieu and certainly attempted to discredit him with the king and possibly even to murder him.

Apparoistra temple luisant orné
La lampe et cierge à Borne et Breteuil
Pour la lucerne le canton destorné
Quand on verra le grand coq au cercueil.

A shining, ornamented temple will appear
The lamp and candle at Borne, and Breteuil
The canton turns aside because of Lucerne
Then we will see the great cock in his coffin.

Lucerne is the name both of a canton and its capital in central Switzerland. The city is built round the remains of a medieval Benedictine monastery, already a secular college by Nostradamus's time and now the great Hofkirche built from 1633. Is this the shining temple Nostradamus foresaw?

Les vieux chemins seront tous embelis
L'on passera à Memphis somentrée
Le grand Mercure d'Hercules fleur de lis
Faisant trembler terre, mer et contree.

The beaten-up roads will be improved
They will travel to a place like Memphis
The French messenger of Hercules
Will cause land, sea and countryside to tremble.

Memphis was the ancient capital of Egypt during and after the
Ptolemaic Dynasty of 323–30BC. The implication here is that
Versailles, built by Louis XIV to encapsulate the perceived
grandeur of France, is the modern Memphis. Louis XIV (1638–
1715) was renowned not only for the splendour of his court, but
also for the numerous wars fought during his 72-year reign.

1641

Dedans Monech le coq sera receu
Le Cardinal de France apparoistra
Par Logarion Romain sera deceu
Foiblesse à l'aigle, et force au coq naistra.

The French cock will be welcomed in Monaco
The Cardinal of France will appear
He will be let down by the Roman Legation
The eagle will be weak, the cock will be born strong.

The Grimaldi family, originally of Genoa, who have played a part in the history of Monaco for a thousand years, have seen many changes in the fortunes of the principality they rule today. Monaguesque princes were loyal to France until 1524, when allegiance switched to Charles V, King of Spain and Holy Roman Emperor. In 1641 the French cock was welcomed back, as a protector of Monaco, by Grimaldi Honoré II.

Vieux Cardinal par le jeune deceu,
Hors de sa change se verra desarmé,
Arles ne monstres double soit aperceu,
Et Liqueduct et le Prince embausmé.

The old Cardinal will be deceived by the young one
He will lose power, once out of office
Arles, don't let on that you've tumbled to the double
Both Liqueduct and the prince are embalmed.

The supplanting of the aged Cardinal Richelieu by his young protégé, Cinq-Mars. Richelieu (1585–1642), having lost the favour of his sovereign, Louis XIII, resigns. When visiting Arles, however, he acquires a copy of a treaty, signed by Cinq-Mars and the king's brother. Fatally ill, he returns to Paris on a barge in order to make the king aware of Cinq-Mars's treachery. He dies soon after his return, with the king following him five months later. Both were embalmed. Liqueduct means 'one who has travelled by water'.

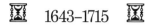 **1643–1715**

De brique en marbre seront les murs reduits
Sept et cinquante annees pacifiques,
Joie aux humains renoué Laqueduict,
Santé, grandz fruict joye et temps melifique.

The walls will go from brick to marble
Fifty-seven peaceful years
Joy to all, the aqueduct renewed
Health, much fruit, joy and happy times.

Following the Battle of the Dunes in 1657, France passed the remaining fifty-seven years of Louis XIV's reign without a single war inside its borders. Louis (1638–1715) was responsible for much building, including the aqueduct canals connecting the Atlantic to the Mediterranean. France did indeed enjoy a golden time under her Sun King.

⌛ 1648 ⌛

Gand et Bruceles marcheront contre Anvers,
Senat de Londres mettront à mort leur Roy,
Le sel et vin luy seront à l'envers,
Pour eux avoir le regne en desarroy.

Ghent and Brussels will march towards Antwerp
The Senate of London will put their King to death
Salt and wine will be turned back to front
Having rights to them will put the realm in disarray.

Peace came to the Low Countries with the 1648 Treaty of Westphalia with Spain. In the following year, the Senate – Parliament – in London executed King Charles I. The cryptic mention of wine and salt is simpler than it looks: King Charles's insistence on his right to levy taxes without reference to Parliament was a prime source of the conflict – and salt and wine are used by Nostradamus to signify taxable commodities.

1649

La forteresse aupres de la Tamise
Cherra par lors le Roi dedans serré
Aupres du pont sera veu en chemise
Un devant mort, puis dans le fort barré.

The fortress near the Thames will fall
When the King is locked inside it
He will be seen in his shirt, near the bridge
One facing death, then locked inside the fort.

A chilling prediction of the execution of King Charles I of England on 30 January 1649. The fallen fortress near the Thames is not the Tower of London, but Windsor Castle, seized by Parliament, where Charles was held until his trial. He went to the block, in shirtsleeves, at Whitehall Palace, within sight of London Bridge.

1649

Plus Macelin que roi en Angleterre
Lieu obscure nay par force aura l'empire
Lasche sans foi, sans loi saignera terre,
Son temps approche si presque je soupire.

More of a butcher than a king of England
Born in obscurity, he will seize the kingdom
A coward with no faith, the lawless land will bleed
I sigh, because his time is so near.

This certainly applies to Oliver Cromwell (1599–1658), whom Nostradamus would have regarded as a Protestant heretic. Born in obscurity, he was known as 'the butcher of Drogheda' after he stormed the Irish town of the same name in 1649 and massacred all its inhabitants. The reference to coward in line 3 may refer to Cromwell's habit of wearing a chain-link shirt out of fear of assassination.

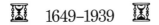

Sept fois changer verrez gent Britannique
Taintz en sang en deux cents nonante an:
Franche non point par appuy Germanique,
Aries doubte son pole Bastarnien.

The British nation will see seven changes
Over two hundred and ninety bloodstained years
German support will not bring freedom
Aries brings fear for Poland.

Starting with the decapitation of King Charles I and the creation of a republic (called the Commonwealth) in 1649, two hundred and ninety years takes Britain's bloodstained history, unnervingly, to the declaration of war on Germany in 1939, following Hitler's invasion of Poland (Bastarnien). Aries is taken by astrologers to refer to the Zodiacal sign of the ram. But Nostradamus will also have known *aries* as the Latin for battering ram – in the language of the Nazis, the *Blitzkrieg*.

 **1650**

La bande faible la terre occupera,
Ceux qui haut lieu ferant horribles cris,
Le gros trouppeau d'estra coin troublera,
Tombe près Dinebro descouvers les escrits.

The weaker army will hold the field
Men of the highlands will make horrible cries
The larger force will be cornered
Falling near Edinburgh, the plans discovered.

Oliver Cromwell's bid to subjugate the Scots very nearly ended in disaster when his army was cornered by a large force of baying Highlanders at Dunbar in September 1650. Brilliant generalship earned Cromwell a surprise victory, gaining him control of Edinburgh.

Le sang du Juste par Taurer la daurade,
Pour se venger contre les Saturnines
Au Nouveau lac plongeront la Maynade,
Puis mercheront contre les Albanins.

The blood of the just shed for the church
For vengeance against the Saturnines
Will plunge into a new lake of blood
Then march against the English.

This cryptic quatrain has been held since the eighteenth century to describe the raising of an army in Scotland by supporters of King Charles II of England following his father's execution. But the new army was defeated in bloody battle by Oliver Cromwell at Worcester on 3 September 1651.

1651

Regne en querelle aux frères divisé,
Prendre les armes et le nom Britannique,
Titre Anglican sera tard avisé
Surprins de nuict mener à l'air Gallique.

The kingdom divided in war between brothers
Takes up arms and the name Britain
The English king will be counselled too late
Surprised and forced by night to seek French air.

A remarkably clear vision of King Charles II's flight to France after the defeat of his army at Worcester in the English Civil Wars. He landed safely in France on 20 October 1651, to begin nine years of exile.

Le Royal sceptre sera contrainct de prendre
Ce que ses predecesseurs avoient engaigé
Puis que l'aneau on fera mal entendre
Lors qu'on viendra le palais saccager.

The Royal sceptre will be forced to take
That which its predecessors had pledged
Because they don't fully understand the ring
When they do come, they sack the palace.

Nostradamus, always sensitive to the fate of royal families, anticipates the interruption of Stuart rule in England on the execution of King Charles I in 1649. Oliver Cromwell, Charles's nemesis, was himself offered the throne by Parliament, but refused it. He disdained the worldly trappings of office, famously saying of the royal sceptre when it was offered him, 'take away that fool's bauble.' The occasion was at the dismissal of the Rump Parliament, 20 April 1653.

La grand peste de cité maritime
Ne cessera que mort ne soit vengée,
Du juste sang par pris damné sans crime,
De la grand dame par feincte n'outragée.

The great plague of the maritime city
Will not cease until death is avenged
For the righteous blood of the condemned innocent
Of the cathedral outraged by false saints.

Nostradamus vows that London will pay the price of plague for the execution of King Charles I in 1649 and for the desecration of churches. The Great Plague struck in the summer of 1665 and killed about 100,000. It subsided only when London was visited with another disaster – the Great Fire of the following year.

Le sang du juste a Londres sera faute
Bruslez par foudres de vingt trois les six,
La dame antique cherra de place haute,
De mesme secte plusieurs seront occis.

The blood of the just will be lacking in London
Burned up in the fire of '66
The ancient lady will topple from her high place
Many of the same sect will be killed.

A prediction of extraordinary accuracy in time. The Great Fire of London destroyed three-quarters of the city in 1666. Eighty-four of the city's one hundred and nine churches (including St Paul's cathedral) were burned, bringing many votive effigies of the Virgin Mary crashing down. But the casualties of the inferno, Christians or otherwise, were fewer than Nostradamus foretold. Only six people died in the fires.

1677

La Soeur aisnée de l'Isle Britannique,
Quinze ans devant le frère aura naissance,
Par son promis, moyennant verrifique,
Succedera au Regne de Balance.

The elder Sister of the British Isle
Aged fifteen, and before her brother's birth
By her promise, being confirmed
Will succeed to the King in a partnership.

Princess Mary, sister of King James II of England, married her cousin, William of Orange, on 4 November 1677 when she was fifteen. William and Mary became joint sovereigns of England – a unique partnership – in 1688, when the autocratic and irrational James II was obliged by Parliament to flee to France.

Seicher de faim, de soif, gent Genevoise,
Espoir prochain viendra au defaillir
Sur point tremblant sera loi Gebenoise.
Classe au grand port ne se peut acuillir.

Desiccated by hunger and thirst, the people of Geneva
Will see their urgent hopes come to nothing
The law of the Cevennes will tremble on the precipice
The fleet cannot find shelter at the great port.

A reference to Nostradamus's favourite *bête noire*, John Calvin.
Calvin lived in the Cevennes, and had enormous influence
there. When Louis XIV revoked the Edict of Nantes in 1685, the
Cevennois revolted. It is certainly conceivable that their
Calvinist allies in Geneva might have sent ships to their aid,
although this is hard to prove.

1688

Le blond au nez forchu viendra commettre,
Par le duelle et chassera dehors
Les exilés, dedans fera remettre,
Aux lieux marins commettant les plus fors.

The blond man will fight the hook-nosed one
In a duel, driving him out
The exiles will return, restoring the status quo
The strongest will be chosen for sea duties.

The blond man is William of Orange, who drove England's James II out of office in 1688. The exiled Stuarts rallied behind their leader, who was sheltering in Ireland, aided by the French fleet. They almost won, but their hopes of a restoration were dashed when William III won the Battle of the Boyne. James fled to France, never to return. The British fleet finally triumphed over the French at Cap La Hague, in 1692.

⧗ 1688–9 ⧗

Trente de Londres secret conjureront,
Contre leur Roi sur le pont entreprinse,
Lui, satalites la mort degousteront.
Un Roi esleu blonde, natif de Frize.

Thirty Londoners, in secret, will conspire
Against their king; the plan will come by sea
He and his courtiers are disgusted by death
The elected king will be fair; a native of Friesland.

The events leading up to the accession to the English throne of
Wiliam III of Orange (1650–1702) in the Glorious Revolution of
1688–9. Married to Mary, daughter of James II, current holder of
the kingship, William insisted that the English nobles who
supported his cause sign their names to a piece of paper before
he would set sail with his fleet. James II, not wishing to die, fled
to France, upon hearing that the commander of his army, the
Duke of Marlborough, had deserted his cause.

🏛 1689 🏛

Le second chef de regne d'Annemarc,
Par Ceux de Frise et l'isle Britannique,
Fera despendre plus de cent mille marc,
Vain exploicter voyage en Italique.

The second chief of the kingdom of Mark Anthony
Because of the Friesians and the British
Will be forced to spend more than 100,000 marks
In a vain attempt to reach Italy.

William of Orange (1650–1702) came from Friesland, and took the throne of England as William III, in 1689. The reference to Mark Anthony is metaphorical, implying the taking over of a foreign kingdom, just as Anthony did, in 33BC Egypt. The figure of 100,000 may refer to the number of French soldiers Louis XIV sent across the border against the Dutch in 1672, which directly led to William's election as captain-general, and to his ultimate accession to the English throne.

De l'aquilon les efforts seront grands.
Sus l'Occean sera la porte ouverte
Le regne en l'isle sera reintegrand,
Tremblera Londres par voille descouverte.

From the North, great efforts will be made
The doors will open over the ocean
On the island, dominion will be restored
London, fearful of the fleet, will tremble.

William of Orange (1650–1702), king of England. The British fleet was harried by the French in naval actions off Beachy Head and at Bantry Bay. William's main strength, however, lay in his land army, which allowed him to confirm his dominion at the Battle of the Boyne, in 1690. The last line may refer back to William's leading of a Dutch fleet up the Thames in 1667, on a raid.

Predictions of Nostradamus for the
16th CENTURY

Etant assis, de nuit secrette étude,
Seul, repose sur la selle d'airan,
Flambe exigue, sortant de solitude,
Fait proferer qui n'est à croire vain.

Seated in my private study at night
Alone at rest on my brass stool
A tiny flame relieves the loneliness
My prophecies will be credible.

Nostradamus embarks on his prophecies, secluded in the new room he had added as an extra storey to his house in Salon. Seated on the prophet's brass stool, he is ready to receive inspiration.

⧗ 1555 ⧗

La verge en main mise au milieu de branches
De l'Onde il mouille et le limbe et le pied:
Un peur et voix fremissent par les manches,
Splendeur divine, Le Divin près s'assied.

With divining rod in the midst of the tree
He finds water at root and branch.
A voice makes me quake with fear
God, in divine splendour, is at hand.

Nostradamus uses the metaphor of the tree of life. Climbing into its branches, he dowses for the water of inspiration – and is aware of the closeness of God.

Le divin verbe donrra à la substance,
Comprins ciel, terre, or occult au laict mystique
Corps, ame esprit ayant toute puissance
Tant soubs ses pieds comme au siege Celique.

The seer will give meaning to the substance
Comprising heaven, earth, alchemist's gold
    and mystic deeds
Body, soul and spirit will be all-powerful
In Hell, just as in Heaven's seat.

This should be read in conjunction with the preceding
quatrains, and taken as an integral part of Nostradamus's
articles of faith. It describes the disembodied and trance-like
state needed to foretell the future, and rightly emphasises the
alchemistical influences that Nostradamus kept so well hidden
from the ruling Catholic church.

⧗ **1555** ⧗

Legis Cantio Contra Ineptos Criticos

Quos legent hosce versus maturé censunto,
Profanum vulgus, et inscium ne attrectato
Omnesq; Astrologi Blenni, Barbari procul sunto,
Qui alter facit, is ritè, sacer esto.

The Law Will Be Invoked Against Inept Critics

May those who read this verse consider it carefully
Let the profane and ignorant keep their distance
Astrologers, idiots and barbarians too, stay away
He who does not, let him be sacred.

Nostradamus rails against ignorant commentators on his work
in his own lifetime and thereafter. Whoever reads this book shall
be considered sacred. Debunkers beware.

Le Roi rusé entendra ses embusches
De trois quartiers ennemis affaillir
Un nombre estranges larmes de coqueluches
Viendra Lemprin du traducteur faillir.

The crafty king is a master of ambush strategy
Enemies threaten from three sides
The hooded ones cry many dubious tears
The translator's borrowing fails.

Nostradamus himself is the crafty king. His three enemies are the church, army and government. Capuchin monks weep crocodile tears as they refute his prophecies – the first among many who will misinterpret them in future.

Le prochain fils de l'aisnier parviendra
Tant esleue jusque au regne des fors
Son apre gloire un chacun la craindra
Mais ses enfans du regne gettez dehors.

The next son of L'Aisnier will succeed
Raised high to great privilege
Everyone will fear his bitter fame
But his children will be ejected from the kingdom.

This quatrain is one of very few written at the request of one of
Nostradamus's patrons, a landowner called L'Aisnier, who asked
the seer (unwisely perhaps) to tell him the fate of his children.

⧗ 1555 ⧗

Apres de France la victoire navale
Les Barchinons, Saillinons, les Phocens
Lierre d'or, l'enclume serré dedans la basle
Ceux de Ptolon au fraud seront consens.

After the French naval victory
People from Barcelona, Salon and Marseilles
The gold-robber, an anvil enclosed in a ball
Men from Toulon are party to the fraud.

An unusual mention for Salon, the town where Nostradamus spent his last years, including those dedicated to writing *The Centuries.* The line suggest a cryptic solution to a crime.

⧗ 1566 ⧗

La synagogue sterile sans nul fruit
Sera receu entre les infideles
De Babylon la fille du porsuit
Misere et triste lui trenchera les aisles.

The sterile synagogue, bearing no fruit
Will be taken by the infidels
The daughter of the persecuted Babylonian
Miserable and sad, her wings will be clipped.

Persecuted by the Christian Church in much of sixteenth-century Europe, Jews were latterly offered the hospitality of Islam in Constantinople and Salonika by Suleiman the Magnificent, Sultan of Turkey. Nostradamus, a Jew by race rather than religion (his family was forcibly converted to Catholicism before his birth) rightly predicted the paradoxical fate of so many of his people.

347

La saincteté trop faincte et seductive,
Accompaigné d'une langue diserte
Lacité vieille et Parme trop hastive,
Florence et Sienne rendront plus desertes.

Sanctity, both faint and too seductive
Accompanied by an agile tongue
The old city and Parma are too hasty
Florence and Siena will become more desert-like.

A pun on Saint Catherine and her namesake, the unsaintly Catherine de Medici. Both Florence and Siena were devastated during the pre-1555 Habsburg-Valois Wars, and Nostradamus is here predicting further trouble between the cities, which indeed continued.

Ignare envie au grand Roi supportee,
Tiendra propos deffendre les escripitz
Sa femme non femme par un autre tentee,
Plus double deux ne fort ne criz.

Ignorant envy is tolerated by the great king
He will propose a ban on writing
His wife, no wife she, will be tempted by another
The treacherous couple will no longer complain
    so loudly.

Nostradamus is here complaining about his treatment by Henri II and his mistress, Diane de Poitiers. Henri lost his life in a joust while wearing Diane's colours – something which must have pleased Nostradamus, as he foretold the tragic event in another quatrain four years before it happened.

1555–6

Par la discorde negligence Gauloise,
Sera passaige á Mahommet ouvert
De sang trempé la terre et mer Senoise,
Le port phocen de voiles et nefs convert.

Due to French discord and negligence
An opportunity will be afforded the Mohammedans
The country and coast of Siena will be soaked in blood
And the port of Marseilles will groan with ships.

Normally taken to imply a future Islamic invasion of Europe,
this quatrain more likely refers to the Habsburg/Valois Italian
Wars of 1555–6. Henri II encouraged his erstwhile ally, Suleiman
the Magnificent (1496–1566), to attack Elba. Suleiman attacked
Piombino, near Siena, instead, much to Henri's disgust, as the
island was an ally of the French.

Quand seront proches de defaut des lunaires,
De l'un à l'autre ne distant grandement,
Froid, siccité, danger vers les frontieres,
Mesme ou l'oracle a prins commencement.

When the moonstruck ones are near defeat
They will be close, one to the other
Cold, drought and danger at the borders
Even at the source of the oracle.

This relates to Nostradamus himself, and to the reaction he
expected from the publication of his prophecies, most notably
from the Huguenots. During December 1556–7 a very severe
winter did indeed follow on from a drought-ridden summer.
Add to that the threatened Spanish invasion of Picardy, and the
quatrain is well-dated.

⧗ 1557 ⧗

Verceil, Milan donra intelligence
Dedans Tycin sera faite la paye
Courir par Siene eau, sang, feu par Florence
Unique choir d'hault en bas faisant maie.

Vercelli, Milan will break the news
The pay-off will be in Pavia
Water, blood and fire from Florence will flow past Siena
The 'one' will fall from high to low shouting for help.

Cosimo de Medici, Duke of Florence, took possession of Siena
on 19 July 1557. In the preceding years, the Sienese had resisted
with great bravery but were brought low by lack of help,
particularly from France.

Le grand mené captif d'estrange terre
D'or enchainé ay Roy Chyren offert
Qui dans Ausone, Milan perdra la guerre
Et tout son ost mis à feu et à fer.

The great man is captured by a strange people
Chained in gold, he is offered to King Chyren
The same man will lose the war in Milan and Ausonia
His entire army will be put to fire and the sword.

Chyren is Nostradamian code for Henry. The great man is
Anne, Duke of Montmorency, who served Henri II of France as
his commanding officer in the wars against the Huguenot forces
of the Prince de Condé and against the Spanish. He was taken
prisoner by the Spaniards, who put his entire force to the sword
at the battle of St Quentin in 1557, but was released at the request
of the king.

Freres et soeurs en divers lieux captifs,
Se trouveront passer pres du monarque
Les contempler ses rameaux ententifs,
Desplaisant voir menton, front, nez, les marques.

Brothers and sisters, imprisoned in different places
Will have the monarch pass close by them
His heirs will look at them attentively
He is displeased to see the marks on their foreheads,
    chin and noses.

In September 1557, Henri II went to view some Huguenot prisoners recently captured in a raid, taking his children with him. He was deeply angered at the marks of brutality visible on the prisoner's faces, and sternly upbraided their captors.

Entrée profonde par la grand Roine faicte
Rendra le lieu puissant inaccessible
L'armee des trois lions sera deffaite,
Faisant dedans cas hideux et terrible.

A deep entry will be made by the great queen
The place will become inaccessible and powerful
The three lion army will be defeated
Causing a hideous and terrible occurrence within.

This may relate to the English loss of Calais in 1558, when it was recaptured by the Duke de Guise for France. The three lions in line 3 refers to a device on the English royal standard of Queen 'bloody' Mary Tudor (1516–1558).

Sur le milieu du grand monde la rose
Pour nouveaux faicts sang public espandu
A dire vrai on aura bouche close
Lors au besoing viendra tard l'attendu.

There is a rose in the middle of the great earth
Because of new deeds, public blood is shed
To be honest, their mouths will be closed
Then, when needed, the long-awaited one will be late.

The rose, insignium of the Tudors, is blamed by Nostradamus for intrigues and crimes in the wider world. The diplomacy of Queen Elizabeth I (reigned 1558–1603), who was promised in marriage to the sovereigns of both France and Spain at different times, was indeed successful in manipulating continental powers to the benefit of England. Nostradamus will have known the Queen's reputation well, and no doubt understood that she would keep her suitors waiting a very long time indeed.

 **1558**

La naturelle à si hault hault non bas
Le tard retour fera marris contens,
Le Recloing ne sera sans debatz
En empliant et pendant tous son temps.

The bastard girl, so very high, not low at all
A late return will make those who regret happy
There will be disputes about the Reconciled One
In filling, and during all of his time.

The bastard girl is Elizabeth Tudor, Elizabeth I of England. Pope Pius IV declared her illegitimate due to the perceived illegality of her mother Anne Boleyn's marriage to Henry VIII. Line 2 shows the Pope (the Reconciled One) changing his mind, then changing it back again. The upshot was that Henry VIII annexed the abbeys and monasteries of England for the benefit of his Royal Treasury, and Elizabeth, his daughter, became one of her country's greatest queens.

L'election faite dans Frankfort
N'aura nul lieu Milan s'opposera
Le sien plus proche semblera si grand fort
Que outre le Rhin és mareschz chassera.

The election which happened in Frankfurt
Will not be allowed, Milan will oppose it
The closest ally will seem so very strong
That he will drive him into the marshes,
  beyond the Rhine.

Ferdinand I (1503–1564) was crowned Holy Roman Emperor in Frankfurt on 24 March 1558. The Pope, Paul IV would not recognise him, but conveniently died in the following year and was replaced by Pius IV, who was more compliant. The Emperor devoted his brief reign to trying to sort out religious wars in Germany – with scant success.

La vraie flamme engloutira la dame
Que voudra mettre les Innocens à feu
Pres de l'assaut l'excercite s'enflamme
Quant dans Seville monstre en boeuf sera veu.

The true flame will swallow up the lady
Who wishes to burn the Innocents
Before the assault the army is inflamed
When in Seville a monstrous ox is seen.

Nostradamus, never favourable towards Queen Elizabeth I of England, seems to have assumed that she, like her elder sister Queen Mary I (1516–58) whom she succeeded, would burn at the stake hundreds of Christians unwilling to deny the 'true' faith. Elizabeth did no such thing. The army mentioned could be one of any number of invasion forces prepared against England, and the monstrous ox an allusion, perhaps, to the notorious beef-eating habits of the British.

Au chef du monde le grand Chyren sera,
Plus oultre apres aimé, craint, redoubté
Son bruit et loz les cieux surpassera,
Et du seul titre victeur fort contenté.

Great Chyren will be leader of the world
Loved, feared, and dreaded, after the 'ne plus ultra'
His fame and praises will reach beyond the heavens
He will be satisfied with the simple title of 'victor'.

This was intended to flatter Henri II (1519–1558). Nostradamus
needed to be in his good graces to survive the Inquisition. He
implies here that Henri will become greater even than Charles V
(1500–1558), Holy Roman Emperor and the 'ne plus ultra' of line
2. Perhaps Nostradamus hoped Henri, flattered into imbecility
by his comparisons, would forget the verse that accurately
predicted his death in a joust.

⧖ 1559 ⧖

Le lion jeune le vieux surmontera,
En champ bellique par singulier duelle
Dans caige d'or les yeux lui crevera,
Deux classes une, puis mourir, more cruelle.

The younger lion will overcome the older
In single combat, on the field of war
His eyes will be pierced in their golden helm
Two breaks made one. He subsequently dies a cruel death.

A foretelling of the death of Henri II, King of France, on 10 July 1559. In a tournament to celebrate the forthcoming double marriage of his sister and his daughter to the Duke of Savoy and King Philip II of Spain, Henri faced Gabriel de Lorge, Count of Montgomery and captain of his Scottish guard. The two men's lances both splintered on contact, that of Montgomery entering the king's gilt helmet and puncturing his head, just above the eye. The king died, in agony, ten days later, throwing the future of France into confusion.

Par le grand Prince limitrophe du Mans
Preux et vaillant chef de grand excercite
Par mer et terre de Gallotz et Normans,
Caspre passer Barcelone pillé isle.

The great prince who borders Le Mans
The gallant and brave leader of the army
Will cross land and sea with the Bretons and Normans
They will pass Barcelona and Gibraltar to pillage the
island.

A 'conditional', or 'retroactive' quatrain in which Nostradamus speculates on what would have happened if Henri II had not been accidentally killed in a joust. Claude de Guise, Henri's cousin, held all the lands around Le Mans, and Nostradamus suggests that instead of wasting his energies against the Protestants, Claude would instead have led a successful invasion against Spain and North Africa.

1559

La paix s'approche d'un costé, et la guerre
Oncques ne feut la pursuitte si grande,
Plaindre homme, femme, sang innocent par terre
Et ce fera de France à toute bande.

Peace comes from one side, war from another
Never before was it so strongly sought after
Pity the men and women, their innocent blood is shed
Throughout the whole of France.

The Treaty of Cateau-Cambrésis was signed on 3 April 1559, effectively ending the wars between France and Spain. Two months later, Henri II was killed in the famous joust predicted by Nostradamus. The Treaty heralded a time of much inter-religious warfare in France, culminating in the bloodbath that was the Massacre of the Huguenots.

🏺 1559 🏺

Les trois pellices de loing s'entrebatron
La plus grand moindre demeurera à l'escoute
Le grand Selin n'en fera plus patron
Le nommera feu peste blanche routte.

The three harlots fight each other from afar
The greater will stay to hear the lesser
Great Selin will no longer be her boss
He will call her fire, plague and white rout.

Perhaps a reference to the three royal mistresses of Henri II. Henri wore Diane de Poitier's colours during his fatal joust with the Count of Montgomery on 10 July 1559. The final line could refer to the king's feelings during his ten-day death agony.

En l'an qu'un oeil en France regnera,
La court sera en un bien dascheux trouble.
Le grand de Bloys son amy tuera,
Le regne mis en mal et doubte double.

In the year France is ruled by a one-eyed man
The court will be very troubled
The great one of Blois will kill his friend
The realm put in harm's way and double uncertainty.

Henry II (1519–59) lived for ten agonised days after the accident which cost him his eye. This event, which Nostradamus had accurately predicted years before, did indeed cast France into a realm of troubles.

⌛ 1559 ⌛

Soubz la colleur du traicte mariage
Fait magnanime par grand Chyren selin
Quintin, Arras recouvrez au voyage
D'espaignolz fait second banc macelin.

Under the glue of a marriage settlement
Great Chyren Selin does a magnificent act
Quintin and Arras are recovered during the journey
A second butcher's table is made by the Spanish.

Nostradamus foresees Henri II (Great Chyren Selin) turning the tables on Spain. Philp II's armies had humiliated the French at St Quentin in 1557 and held the Spanish Netherlands (in which Arras was the principal southern stronghold), where Henri was unsuccessful in an invasion bid in the same year. Henri relinquished his ambitions against Spain in a treaty of 1559 and died in the same year. An unfulfilled prediction.

Les exilez par ire, haine intestine,
Feront au Roy grand conjuration
Secret mettront ennemis par la mine,
Et ses vieux siens contre aux sedition.

Those exiled through anger and internal feuds
Will hatch a great plot against the king
They will place enemies, in secret, by threats
And the king's followers will be undermined.

This prophecy came true five years after its publication. It tells of the 1560 Conspiracy of Amboise, in which the Bourbons and the Montmorencys conspired to kill the Duke of Guise and kidnap the king, Francis II. The plot was exposed by an informant, leading to the arrest and murder of most of the perpetrators. An outraged De Guise hung their bodies around the walls of Amboise castle.

Bossu sera esleu par le conseil,
Plus hideux monstre en terre n'appareu,
Le coup voulant prelat crevera l'oeil,
Le trasitre au Roy pour fidelle receu.

The hunchback is elected by the council
A more hideous monster never appeared on earth
A direct shot will pierce his eye
This traitor whom the King received in good faith.

The hunchback is the Prince de Condé, arch-conspirator against the throne and the Catholic church, and thus loathed by Nostradamus. He was elected chief of the Huguenot council on 19 March 1560. After many plots against his king, for which he was forgiven more than once, the Prince was captured at the battle of Jarnac in 1569. He was summarily executed with a pistol shot to the head.

⧗ 1560 ⧗

Dedans Lyons vingt et cinq d'une haleine,
Cinq citoyens, Germains, Bressans, Latins,
Par dessous noble conduiront longue train,
Et descouverts par abois de matins.

In Lyons, twenty-five people with a common purpose
Five citizens, with Germans, Bressans and Italians
Below, nobles lay a trail of powder
And are discovered by barking guard dogs.

The conspiracy of September 1560 in which five Lyons citizens, including the Prince de Condé, colluded with foreign Protestants to blow open the gates of the city and allow it to be seized by Huguenots. The plot was discovered by the night watch.

Neuf ans le regne le maigre en paix tiendra
Puis il cherra en soif si sanguinaire
Pour lui grand peuple sans foi et loi mourra
Tué par un beaucoup plus debonnaire.

For nine years the thin man's rule will be peaceful
Then he will fall into such a bloody thirst
A great nation, faithless and lawless, will die for him
Killed by a force much better than himself.

Ivan IV, the Terrible, first Tsar of Russia (1530–1584) was a contemporary monster whose reputation would have been known to Nostradamus. Ivan succeeded as tsar of Muscovy as a child, officially taking the reins of power at twenty-one in 1551. He waged war beyond Muscovy's borders into the wider reaches of Russia, but maintained peace at home until 1560 when his beloved consort, Anastasia, died suddenly. It was at this moment that he became a crazed despot, submitting his realm to terror.

Premier fils veufve malheureux mariage
Sans nuls enfans deux Isles en discord,
Avant dix-huit incompetent age.
De l'autre près plus bas sera l'accord.

The widow's eldest son, unhappy marriage
Without children two Isles in discord
Before eighteen still under age
The next eldest will be betrothed even younger.

The son is Francis II of France, eldest child of Henri II. Married to Mary Queen of Scots when he was fourteen, the sickly Francis fathered no children and died from a tumour in his ear on 5 December 1560, aged only sixteen. Having mothered no heir, Mary returned to Scotland, where she famously did much to put the two Isles (her own kingdom and England) into discord. Francis's younger brother, Charles IX (1550–74), who succeeded him, had become engaged to Elizabeth of Austria in 1561, aged only eleven. The couple did not marry until 1570.

⧗ 1564 ⧗

Puanteur grande sortira de Lausanne,
Qu'on ne seura l'origine du fait,
Lon mettra hors toute le gente loingtaine
Feu veu au ciel, peuple estranger deffait.

A foul stink will come from Lausanne
No one will know what caused it
All foreigners will be driven out
Fire will be seen in the sky, the aliens defeated.

Nostradamus's bitterest rival was Théodore de Bèze (1519–1605), who originally taught Greek at Lausanne before becoming John Calvin's chief disciple. He evolved into the foremost apostle of Calvinism following Calvin's death in 1564, and made no secret of his disdain for '*Monstre*-damus's' inflated prophecies. In a childish response, Nostradamus called him Bèze the 'beast'. '*Bête Noire*' Bèze would have enjoyed debunking this particular prophecy, because it was never fulfilled.

Pont on fera promptement de nacelles,
Passer l'armee du grand prince Belgique
Dans profondres et non loing de Brucelles,
Outre passés, detrenchés sept à picque.

A pontoon bridge will quickly be built
Over which the Belgian prince's army will pass
It will pour forth, not far from Brussels
Once through, seven will be killed by pikes.

The word *Belgique* was archaic when Nostradamus was writing this quatrain, and can only refer to the gift of the Belgae's original tribal territory by Charles V to his son, Philip II, in 1554. An invasion of France was attempted in 1564, using a boat-bridge across the River Scheldt.

🖹 1566 🖹

La Dame seule au regne demeurée
D'unic esteint premier au lict d'honneur,
Sept ans sera de douleur explorée.
Puis longue vie au regne par grand heur.

The Lady is left alone in the kingdom
Her only husband dead on the field of honour
There will be seven years of mourning
Then she will live long, for the kingdom's good.

Catherine de Medici, Henri II's widow, did mourn him for exactly seven years – until 1 August 1566. She lived another twenty-three years, and Nostradamus felt certain she would do nothing but good. His loyalty to her was understandable – she spared his life when members of the court accused him of causing the king's death by predicting it – but misplaced.

 **1566**

Dame à l'absence de son grand capitaine
Sera priee d'amours du Viceroi
Faincte promesse et malheureuse estraine
Entre les mains du grand Prince Barrois.

The lady, in the absence of her great Captain
Will be begged for love favours by the Viceroy
A fraudulent promise, unhappiness in love
She falls into the hands of the Barred Prince.

Diane de Poitiers (1499–1566) was the mistress of Henri II of
France. Twenty years his senior, she nevertheless outlived him,
and after his death in 1559 factions (a Barred prince is one of the
royal line) at court sought to maintain her influence. But she
sensibly withdrew from public life to her château at Anet.

Lettres trouvees de la roine les coffres,
Point de subscrit sans aucun nom d'hauteur
Par la police seront caché les offres,
Qu'on ne scaura qui sera l'amateur.

Letters are found in the queen's cabinet
Without signature, or author's name
The offers are concealed by a ruse
So no one will know who her lover is.

Nostradamus may well have met the fourteen-year-old Mary, Queen of Scots (1542–1587), when he was summoned to the French Court in 1556. Eleven years later, the so-called Casket Letters appeared, purporting to reveal the truth about the murder of the Queen's second husband, Lord Darnley. Following Mary's execution for 'sedition', in 1587, the letters, which may well have been fakes, conveniently disappeared.

Jour que sera par roine saluee
Le jour apres le salut, la priere
Le compte fait raison et valbuee
Par avant humbles oncques ne feut si fiere.

One day she will be greeted by the queen
The next day she will pray
The rendering is right and good
Among humble women, never was there one so proud.

Mary, Queen of Scots (1542–1587), no longer a queen following her abdication in favour of her son James VI in 1567, went to the executioner's block on 8 February 1587. This followed her exile to England in 1568, when she threw herself on the mercy of Elizabeth I. Elizabeth later confined her for life, eventually signing her death warrant when news was brought her that Mary was plotting to usurp the English throne for the Catholics. Mary was in prayer as the axe fell.

Le grand pilot par Roi sera mandé,
Laisser la classe pour plus haut lieu attaindre
Sept ans apres sera contrebandé,
Barbare armée viendra Venise craindre.

The great pilot will be ordered by the king
To leave the fleet, for a higher rank
Seven years later he will revolt
A Barbarian army will cow Venice.

A reference to Gaspard de Coligny (1519–1572), admiral-in-chief of Henri II's fleet. He resigned when the king died, in order to ally himself with the Calvinist party. He became instrumental in fomenting the Huguenot/Catholic wars, which took place at the same time that Suleiman the Magnificent and Selim II were harrying Venice and her possessions in the Mediterranean.

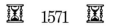

La barbe crespe et noir par engin
Subjugera la gent cruelle et fiere
Le grand Chiren ostera du longin,
Tous les captifs par Seline barriere.

The black and curly-bearded one, by ingenuity
Subdues a fierce and cruel people:
Great Henry will take from far away
All captives of the Turkish banner.

Nostradamus deals with the battle of Lepanto in numerous quatrains. Under Charles X of France, 1500 Christian slaves were freed from enforced service in the Turkish fleet. Henri III only took over the throne in 1574, so Nostradamus would seem to be three years out in his use of Henry, in line 3. However the commander of the crusade against the Turks was a certain Don John of Austria, who was, indeed, dark and bearded.

Au port Selin le tyran mis à mort,
La Liberté non pourtant recouvree
Le nouveau Mars par vindicte et remort
Dame par force de frayeur honoree.

The tyrant will be killed at the port of the crescent moon
Liberty, however, will not be regained
A new war, caused by vengeance and remorse
Will cause Our Lady to be honoured, through fear.

The death of Ali Pasha at the battle of Lepanto, on 7 October 1571, did not signal the end of Turkish aggression in the Mediterranean. It persisted for centuries, leading to the eventual loss of Muslim influence over the region, and a return to the Catholic ascendancy through force of arms.

⧗ 1571 ⧗

Dans les Espaignes viendra Roi trespuissant
Par Mer et terre subjugant or midi
Ce mal fera rabaissant le croissant
Baisser les aesles à ceux du vendredi.

A great king will enter Spain
By sea and land he will subjugate the southern gold
This evil will cause the lowering of the crescent flag
Clipping the wings of the Muslims.

This very clearly applies to Philip II of Spain (1527–1598) who clipped the wings of the Turks at the Battle of Lepanto, and was responsible for ejecting the Moors from Spain in 1571. His power was in large part due to his inheritance of the extensive Spanish colonies in the New World, on which he came to rely for the replenishment of his treasury.

Le Noir farouche quand aura essayé
Sa main sanguine par feu, fer, arcs tendus,
Trestous le peuple sera tant effrayé
Voir les plus grans par col et pieds pendus.

When the ferocious King will have applied
His bloody hand to fire, steel and bowstrings
All the people will be so terrified
To see great men hanged by neck and feet.

A black day in the history of France, St Bartholomew's day, 24 August 1572, saw the massacre of the Huguenots in Paris, carried out at the behest of Catherine de Medici with the consent of the son she dominated, King Charles IX. Note that Nostradamus uses the capitalised Noir as an anagrammatical code for Roi. Aged only twenty-two, Charles not only witnessed the slaughter from a window in the Louvre palace, but joined in by shooting into the crowd. Many Huguenot leaders were hanged in the streets, or had their corpses strung up from gibbets by their feet.

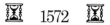

Qui au Royaume Navarrois parviendra
Quand de Sicile et Naples seront joints
Bigore et Landres par Foix loron tiendra
D'un qui d'Espaigne sera par trop conjoint.

He who achieves the kingship of Navarre
When Sicily and Naples become allies
Will hold Bigorre and Landes through Foix and Oloron
From one too strongly allied to Spain.

Henri IV, born in 1553 as Nostradamus was producing his *Centuries*, succeeded to the throne of Navarre in 1572. Henri became the first Bourbon king of France in 1589, and restored the nation, through his pragmatic policies, to peace and stability after 40 years of bitter religious wars.

La pestilence l'entour de Capadille
Un autre faim pres de Sagont s'appreste
Le chevalier bastard de bon senille
Au grand de Thunes fera trancher la teste.

The plague surrounds Capellades
Another famine is threatening Sagunto
The good old man's bastard knight
Will cause the great Tunisian to lose his head.

The recapture of Tunis by Spain in 1573. The good old man is
Charles V (1500–58), King of Spain and Holy Roman Emperor
and his bastard knight his illegitimate son Don John of Austria
(1547–78) who commanded the Spanish forces at Tunis. The
mention of plague is apposite, for Don John died in the
outbreak of 1578.

 **1573**

L'armee de mer devant la cité tiendra
Puis partir sans faire langue alee,
Citoyens grande proie en terre prendra,
Retourner classe, reprendre grand emblee.

The naval contingent will stand before the city
Then leave, without having to go far
Many citizens will be captured, by land
The fleet returns, to seize in a great robbery.

Sir Francis Drake (1540–1596) was responsible for capturing the greatest treasure in the history of piracy when he swooped on a hoard of Spanish silver from the Potosi mines of New Castile, in 1573, just as the ingots were being transported by porters across the Isthmus of Panama prior to their shipment for Spain.

La grand pesche viendra plaindre, plorer
D'avoir esleu, trompés seront en l'aage
Guiere avec eux ne voudra demourer,
Deçeu sera par ceux de son langaige.

The great fish will come to weep and complain
For having chosen, deceit about the age
He will not wish to stay with them
He will be deceived by his own people.

Pesche in line 1 refers to the way the Polish nobility traditionally chose their kings – almost randomly, as if by fishing. Henri III of France (1551–1589) was elected King of Poland in just this way, but threw up the job to return to France on hearing of the unexpected death of his brother, Charles IX, on 30 May 1574. He was himself deceived and killed by a fellow countryman, Jacques Clément, fifteen years later.

1574

Des sept rameaux à trois seront reduicts,
Les plus aisnés seront surprises par mort,
Fratricider les deux seront seduicts,
Les conjures en dormant seront morts.

The seven branches are cut to three
The two elder sons will be surprised by death
Both seduced by fratricide
The conspirators will die in their sleep.

Of the seven children of Henri II, his second son, Charles IX, died in 1574. He was succeeded by the third, Henri III. The next son in line, François Duc d'Alençon, who espoused the Huguenot cause, tried to overthrow his brother in the fratricidal War of the Malcontents from 1574–76. At the end of it all, the original seven were reduced to three.

Celui qu'en luitte et fer au faict bellique,
Aura porté plus grand que lui le prix
De nuict au lict six lui feront la pique,
Nud sans harnois subit sera surprins.

He who, in battle, and warlike action
Shall carry off a prize, greater than himself
Will be attacked at night, in bed, by six men:
Naked, without armour, he will be ambushed.

A reference to the Comte de Montgomery, unwitting killer of King Henri II in a joust in 1559. Although Henri II had pardoned him before his death, Catherine de Medici, Henri's wife, was not so understanding. She put a price on Montgomery's head. He fled to England. Fifteen years later in 1575, he returned to Normandy at the head of a Protestant rebel army. Forced to surrender at Domfront, he was spared, but was kidnapped from his bedroom by six men, on 27 May, and sent to the Conciergerie, where he later died, probably on Catherine's orders.

⧗ 1577 ⧗

Pour le plaisir d'edict voluptueux,
On meslera le poison dans la foy:
Venus sera en cours si vertueux,
Qu'obfusquera du Soleil tout aloy.

For the pleasure of the licentious edict
Poison will mingle into the faith
Venus will be so virtuous at Court
She will obscure the sunlight of righteousness.

In 1577 Henri III issued the Edict of Poitiers, permitting France's Protestants to practise their beliefs, and acknowledging the validity of their clergy's marriages. Nostradamus anticipates this liberalism with obvious disapproval, avowing that the acceptance of these voluptuaries at Court will cast a wicked shadow over the celibate priests of the one true, Roman Catholic, faith.

L'an que Mercure, Mars, Venus retrograde
Du grand Monarque la ligne ne faillit
Esleu du peuple l'usiant pres de Gagdole
Qu'en paix et regne viendra fort envieillir.

In the year when Mercury, Mars and Venus retrograde
The Monarch's family line won't fail
Elected by the Portuguese near Cadiz
He'll reign and grow very old in his peaceful kingdom.

In 1580, King Philip II of Spain succeeded to the throne of
Portugal by virtue of his marriage in 1543 to the Portuguese
infanta Mary (who died three years later giving birth to their
son, Don Carlos). Philip reigned over the twin kingdoms until
his death in 1598, aged seventy-one.

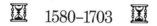 **1580–1703**

En l'an cinq cens octante plus et moins,
On attendra le siecle bien estrange
En l'an sept cens, et trois cieux en tesmoings.
Que plusieurs regnes un à cinq feront change.

In the year fifteen hundred and eighty, give or take
We can expect a very strange century
In the year seventeen hundred and three, as the sky
    will witness
Several kingdoms, one to five, will cause changes.

An accurate and date-specific quatrain. In 1580, France was
fighting a virtual Civil War, known as the 'Seventh War of
Religion'. This effectively began the seventeenth Century, which,
in French terms, lasted until 1703 and Louis XIV's War of the
Spanish Succession. The five Kingdoms mentioned in line 4 are
Spain, the Americas, the Netherlands and the two Sicilys.

1581

De plus grand perte nouvelles raportées,
Le raport fait le camp s'estonnera
Bandes unies encontre revoltées,
Double phalange grand abandonnera.

News of the new great loss is reported
This will astonish the army
War bands unite against the mutineers
A double phalanx will abandon its leader.

This relates to the Dutch capture of Antwerp, in 1581, caused by rumours of a great defeat and possible mutiny spreading through the Duke of Parma's army. The Duke, Alessandro Farnese, only regained Antwerp on 17 August 1585.

La republique de la grande cité
A grand rigueur ne voudra consentir,
Roy sortir hors par trompette cité
L'eschelle au mur, la cité repentir.

The republicans of the great city
Will not wish to accept royal rule
The King, leaving, by a trumpet sound
Swears with ladders to make the city repent.

Paris rebelled against Henri III on 12 May 1588 in the celebrated uprising inspired by the Duke of Guise, whom the Catholic League wished to put on the throne in place of the Huguenot-tolerating incumbent. The rising has become famous in history as the *Journée des Barricades,* in which Parisians lifted the very paving stones from the streets to hurl at the King's supporters. Henri was lucky to escape with his life, swearing revenge. He had Guise murdered, and returned to lay siege to Paris, in the following year.

⌛ 1588 ⌛

Paris conjure un grand meurtre commettre
Blois lefera sortir en plain effet,
Ceux d'Orleans voudront leur chef remettre,
Angers, Troye, Langres leur feront un meffait.

The committing of murder plotted in Paris
Will be carried out openly at Blois
Men of Orleans wish to restore their leader
Angers, Troyes and Langres are with the king.

Henry III vowed to murder the Duke of Guise following the
Paris revolt of May 1588, and carried out his intention at Blois on
25 December of that year. France was divided by this crime:
Orleans came out for Guise; Angers, Troyes and Langres for the
king.

Voille gallere voil de nef cachera,
La grande classe viendra sortir la moindre.
Dix naves proches le tourneront poulser,
Grande vaincue unis à foi joindre.

The sails of the galleys will hide those of smaller ships
The great fleet will call out the smaller one
Ten nearby ships will drive it back
The great one vanquished, to join those united in faith.

The Catholic Spanish Armada of Philip II was sent against the
Protestant Elizabethan English in July 1588. Hopelessly outnum-
bered, the English sent out fire-ships to harass the Spanish.
Driven by contrary winds, the Spanish were then forced to
circumnavigate the British Isles, more than half the fleet
foundering on the Irish shore. Of 130 galleys sent out, only 67
returned. The defeat almost bankrupted the Spanish Royal
treasury.

1588

Un filz du Roi tant de langues aprins,
A son aisné au regne different
Son pere beau au plus grand filz comprins
Fera perir principal adherent.

A king's son, master of many languages
Different from the one who reigned before him
His handsome father will know which son is greater
Causing the main pretender's death.

Henri III (1551–1589) spoke several languages fluently, unlike his brother, Charles IX, whom he succeeded. Henri II was his handsome father – the one who died in a joust – and the last line refers to Henri's murder of the Guises, in 1588.

⌛ 1588 ⌛

De fin porphire profond collon trouvee
Dessoubz la laze escriptz capitolin
Os poil retors Romain force prouvee,
Classe agiter ay port de Methelin.

A deep vein of finest porphyry is discovered
Beneath the inscriptions at the base of the capitol
Bones, hair, the return of an already proved Italian army
Mutiny at the port of Mitylene.

Ancient Mitylene was once the capital of Lesbos. In 1588 a large,
rose-granite obelisk was discovered in the Basilica of St Peter in
Rome. Its finding coincided, fortuitously for Nostradamus, with
an invasion of Lesbos.

🏺 1588 🏺

Par la fureur d'un qui attendra l'eau
Par la grand raige tout l'exercite esmeu
Chargé des nobles à dix sept bateaulx
Au long du Rosne, tard messagier venu.

The fury of a man waiting for the water
His great rage causes the army to move
Seventeen ships loaded with nobles
The belated messenger travels the length of Rhone.

Poor intelligence (belated messenger) made Philip of Spain's naval Armada against England in 1588 a doomed venture. Enraged by continual attacks on his navy, in harbour as well as on the high seas, by privateers such as Sir Francis Drake, Philip ordered his commander, the Duke of Medina Sidona, to set sail inadequately prepared for the mission. In total, after the four-month voyage, the fleet lost no less than sixty-five ships including many full of troops under aristocratic command.

1588

Le ranc Lorrain fera place à Vendosme
Le hault mis bas et le bas mis en hault
Le filz d'Hamon sera esleu dans Rome
Et les deux grands seront mis en deffault.

The House of Lorraine will give way to Vendôme
The high will become low, the low high
The son of Ham will be elected in Rome
And the two great ones will be in the wrong.

This is probably a reference to the murder of the two de Guise brothers by Henri III, on 23 December 1588. Henri de Guise had usurped the throne of France that year, with the help of the Catholic League against the Protestants. The son of Ham would imply a black pope; something that has yet to occur.

Par lors qu'un Roi sera contre les siens,
Natif de Blois subjugera Ligures.
Mammel, Cordube et les Dalmatiens,
Des sept puis l'ombre à Roi estrennes et lemurs.

When a king turns against his own people
A native of Blois will conquer the Genoese
Mammola, Cordoba and the Dalmatians
The seven, then the shadow will give the king
money and ghosts.

Nostradamus's code for Henri III is 'Blois', after his country residence. Lines 2 and 3 are more difficult to analyse but line 4 returns to Catherine de Medici's seven children. The shadow may refer to the king's murder of the Duke of Guise and of his brother on 25 December 1588, which took place, coincidentally, at Blois.

Le grand empire sera par Angleterre
Le pempotam des ans plus de trois cens,
Grandes copies passer par mer et terre,
Les Lusitains n'en seront pas contens.

The great empire will be made by England,
All-powerful for more than three hundred years
Great forces will move by sea and land
The Portuguese will not be happy.

Nostradamus foresees the British Empire, dating its ascendancy from the Spanish Armada in July 1588. This naval disaster, in which Spain lost 10,000 men and fifty-six ships, ended Spain's supremacy and handed sea power to Britain. The Empire did last for three hundred years until its progressive dismantling in the twentieth century. The Portuguese were firm allies of Britain for much of that era, but back in 1588 had been in an unwise alliance with Spain.

1589

Par la response de dame Roy troublé,
Ambassadeurs mespriseront leur vie,
Le grand ses frères contrefera double,
Par deux mourront, ire, haine et envie.

By agreeing with the disturbed king's mother
Ambassadors risked their lives
The great man will take his brothers' places
The two will die by anger, loathing and fear.

Henry III's mother, Catherine de Medici, was horrified at her
son's complicity in the assassination of the Duke of Guise in
1588. Her reaction was openly shared by leading Catholic
noblemen, among them the Duc de Mayenne, who bravely took
the helm of the Catholic League in place of his two brothers,
respectively the Duke and Cardinal of Guise.

🏳 1589 🏳

De Flora issue de sa mort sera cause,
Un temps devant par jeune et vieille bueira,
Par les trois lys lui feront telle pause,
Par son fruit sauve comme chair crue mueire.

Flowers will be the cause of her death
Once, soon, by young and old, it will be drunk
The three lilies will make her pause for so long
That her children will be saved, just as the meat
  is dampened.

Catherine de Medici came from a family of renowned poisoners, but she actually died of pneumonia, in 1589. She married into the lilies of France, becoming Henri II's queen. Florence, which is another possible meaning for 'Flora' in line 1, was the capital city of the Medici Duchy of Tuscany.

⧗ 1589 ⧗

Dans le millieu de la forest Meyenne,
Sol au lyon la fouldre tombera.
Le grand bastard issu du Grand du Maine,
Ce jour fougeres pointe en sang entrera.

In the middle of the Mayenne forest
With the Sun in Leo, lightning will strike
The famous bastard, son of the Maine man
On that day the sword of Fougères will enter his blood.

Fougères, 20 miles from the forest of Mayenne, was once the ancestral home of a great family of the same name which died out in the thirteenth century. Henri III used the house while he was still Duke of Anjou. He was to die in August 1589, stabbed by an assassin in his bedchamber at Saint-Cloud.

Ce que fer, flamme n'a sceu paracheuer,
La douce langue an conseil viendra faire
Par repos, songe, le Roy fera resver,
Plus l'ennemy en feu, sang militaire.

What iron and flame cannot achieve
Sweet words, in council, will contrive
Imagine this; the King, while resting, will not dream
That the enemy at his hearth has military blood.

Henri III of France (1551–89) was stabbed in the stomach and killed by a young Dominican monk named Jacques Clément (the *douce langue* of Nostradamus's quatrain), on 2 August 1589. Three days before his death, Henri had dreamed that his royal emblems would be trodden underfoot by monks, leading the common people.

Sang Royal fuis, Monhurt, Mas, Equillon
Remplis seront de Bourdelois les landes
Navarre, Bigorre poinctes et eguillons
Profondz de faim vorer de liege glandes.

Flight of the blood royal, Monheurt, Agen, Aguillon
The lands of the Bordelais will be full
Navarre and Bigorre, with point and spur
Starving, they eat the cork oak acorns.

Only Navarre (in Spain) lies outside the region of southwest France where all the other named towns are located. An allusion to Henri of Navarre (1553–1610) and his struggles for the French throne, which he claimed on the assassination of Henri III in 1589.

L'ombre du Regne de Navarre non vrai,
Fera la vie de fort illegitime
La veu promis incertain de Cambrai
Roi Orleans donra mur legitime.

There is a false shadow over the kingdom of Navarre
It will cast doubts on the life of the strong one
An uncertain vow made at Cambrai
The King of Orleans restores the legitimate border.

There were doubts as to Henri IV of Navarre's rights of succession after the murder of Henri III in 1589. He did, however, bring a measure of stability back to France after the depredations of the Wars of Religion. He had many mistresses, one the wife of Balagny, governor of Cambrai. Line 3 may describe his gift to Balagny of hereditary possession of the town. Line 4 may simply refer to the 1598 Edict of Nantes, which demarcated the 'legitimate border' between Catholic and Protestant in France.

Ne sera soul jamais de demander
Grand Mendosus obtiendra son Empire
Loing de la cour fera contremander
Pimond, Picard, Paris, Tyrron le pire.

There will be no one left to ask
Great Mendosus will attain his empire
Far from the court, he will countermand
Piedmont, Picardy, Paris, and Tuscany the worst.

Mendosus applies to the family of Vendôme, and, in particular, to Henri IV of Navarre, who finally attained the kingship of France in 1589, after a long struggle. He was responsible for the Edict of Nantes in 1598, giving political rights to French Protestants and effectively countermanding the endless lobbying of the Catholic League.

De l'Orient viendra le coeur punique,
Fascher Adrie, et les hoirs Romullides,
Accompagne de la classe Libique
Trembler Melites et proches Isles vuides.

From the east will come a treacherous heart
To trouble Hadrian and the heirs of Romulus
Accompanied by the Libyans
To shake Melites and the nearby empty islands.

Henri of Navarre (Hadrian) had to quit the siege of Paris in September 1590 at the approach of the Duke of Parma. The 'heirs of Romulus' refers to the Vatican, which supported Henri against Parma's sovereign, Philip II of Spain.

Amour alegre non loing pose le siege
Au Sainct barbare seront les garrisons.
Ursins, Hadrie, pour Gaulois feront plaige,
Pour peut rendus de l'Armée, aux Grisons.

The eager lover will not impose a long siege
The garrisons will be profane clergy
Hadrian will spare street children for France
So they can serve the army, until grey-beards.

Another reference to Henri of Navarre's brief and unsuccessful siege of Paris. Nostradamus sees Henri (again called Hadrian – see preceding quatrain) as a forward-looking man who is careful not to alienate the urchins of the city, recognising that they can become soldiers and live long. Describing Henri as the eager lover can only be a reference to the lurid affair the king was having with Gabrielle d'Estrées throughout the siege.

Le circuit du grand faict ruineux,
Le nom septiesme du cinquiesme sera
D'un tiers plus grand l'estrange belliqueux,
Mouton, Lutece, Aix ne garantira.

The disastrous act is accomplished
The seventh name will now be the fifth
A third greater, this foreign warmonger
Will not manage to keep Paris and Aix in Aries.

The fifth child of Henri II and Catherine de Medici, Henri III became the seventh and last king of the Valois line. Henri IV, Prince of Navarre, who succeeded him, was considered a foreigner, as Navarre was at that time deemed to be unconnected to France. The first line must refer to the Massacre of St Bartholomew's Day, which heralded the end of the Valois line. The last line may indicate Henri de Navarre's siege of Paris in March and April (Aries) of 1590.

Les Nictobriges par ceux de Perigort
Seront vexez tenant jusques au Rosne
L'associé de Gascons et Begorne
Trahir le temple, le prebstre estant au prosne.

The Agenais will be troubled by the Perigourdiens
All the way to the Rhone
The man who associates with both Gascons and Bigorres
Will betray the church, even as the priest delivers his sermon.

The religious wars of southern France were a constant background in Nostradamus's own lifetime. Here he envisions a Protestant linked to Gascony who betrays the (Catholic) church. He may be visualising the future doctrinal pragmatism of the future Protestant Henri of Navarre, who did so much to bridge the religious divide by adopting the Catholic faith before his coronation with the immortal words '*Paris vaut bien une messe*' (Paris is well worth a mass). Nostradamus, a devout Catholic, would not have approved.

Mandosus tost viendra à son hault regne
Mettant arriere un peu de Nolaris
Le rouge blaisme, le masle à l'interregne
Le jeune crainte et frayeur Barbaris.

Mandosus will soon have his great reign
Setting aside, somewhat, those of Nolaris
The pale red one, he of the interregnum
The young man fears the barbaric terror.

If Mandosus is Vendôme, and Nolaris is Lorraine, this quatrain tells of Henri IV's accession in 1594 and the consequent decline of the house of Guise. The pale red one must be the aged Cardinal de Bourbon, later declared King Charles X, who only reigned for a year, dying in 1590. Masle would then be the Duke de Mayenne, and the young man the Duke of Guise. Barbaris refers to Philip II of Spain, who laid claim to the French throne through his daughter, Isabella.

Chassez seront sans faire long combat,
Par le pais seront plus fort grevés,
Bourg et Cité auront plus grand debat,
Carcas, Narbonne auront coeurs éprouvés.

Chased away without a long fight
They will be sorely burdened by the peace
Town and city will have a great discussion
Carcas and Narbonne will prove their hearts.

Carcas is Carcassonne, the fortified medieval city of the Aude in southwest France. Well-known to Nostradamus, the city gave itself up to the sovereignty of Henri IV in 1596 after changing hands several times during the century's religious wars. Narbonne, nearby, had a similar history. In Nostradamus's day, as now, these ancient cities were administratively divided into the original *cité* and the *bourg*, or new town.

⧗ 1596 ⧗

Devant le lac ou plus cher fut getté
De sept mois, et son host desconfit
Seront Hispans par Albanois gastez
Par delai perte en donnant le conflict.

In front of the lake where the treasure was lost
The army was routed, for seven months
The Spanish will be harassed by the English
They will delay the battle, and thus lose.

Captains Essex, Howard and Raleigh attacked a Spanish treasure
fleet in Cadiz, in June 1596. The forty galleons and thirteen
warships had just completed a seven-month voyage from the
newly conquered territories of South and Central America. All
were destroyed. Nostradamus obviously foresaw the coming
war between England and Spain, who, at the time of writing,
were allies, due to a marriage which had been contracted
between Mary Tudor, Queen of England, and Philip II of Spain.